# Feelings
## and
# Faith

*Reflections on God's Gifts for Life's Journey*

Dana - special journey friend!
Embrace YOUR FEELINGS for Good,
Trust FAITH along your journey days.
Lou

Louis W. Accola

*Louis W. Accola*

ISBN 978-1-63630-692-6 (Paperback)
ISBN 978-1-63630-693-3 (Hardcover)
ISBN 978-1-63630-694-0 (Digital)

Covenant Books, Inc.
11661 Hwy 707
Murrells Inlet, SC 29576
www.covenantbooks.com

In memory of all my global sisters and brothers whose life journey was ended by COVID-19; in gratitude for the courageous love, compassion, care, and sacrifice given by all doctors, nurses, support staff, and all first responders, including police and community leaders who risked and sacrificed so much of their lives during the COVID-19 pandemic; and in joy for my family, friends, and all in God's global family who are fortunate to continue their life journeys.

# Contents

# Preface

This book was first written for the purpose and in the format of a ten weeks sermon series on the topic of "Feelings and Faith" that was preached in the congregation I was serving at the time. I decided to transform this sermon series into a book while I was hunkered down in our retirement cottage in the Valley of the Sun in Mesa, Arizona. Following the strict confinement guidelines during the COVID-19 pandemic gave me both the time and solitude for this project. I only went outdoors for walking my dog Lexi and my exercise as a part of my self-care and soul-care routine. No visitors were allowed into our cottage for months. This confinement and book project was only interrupted for essential outings to get meds and some basic groceries like milk, bread, eggs, and a couple of large cartons of Drumstick Ice Cream. Our cottage is located in Maricopa County, which was in the hot spot for coronavirus in Arizona. All the feelings considered in this book were especially being experienced at that threatening time in my life's journey during the COVID-19 pandemic.

We are created in God's image. We each express in our own being the presence, nature, and attributes that we see in the God we encounter in the Old Testament and in the life story of Jesus (Word became flesh) recorded in the four Gospels that we have in the New Testament. We are by God's design creatures of feelings. Our feelings are seen in the encounters, experiences, and journey with this living God in these accounts and in Jesus's life. Our feelings are neither good nor bad. In God's design, our feelings are in the "makeup package" of our natural essence as living beings. Our feelings are to be expressed through each of our unique personalities and spiritualities. It is how we see them, understand them, express them, and control them as responsible selves that counts in life's journey. These feelings are both, in our freedom "to be" and "to act," potentially either good or bad. Created in the image of God means that these feeling are gifts in our designed beings to be affirmed, expressed, and shared.

These feelings are sometimes associated with weakness, broken-ness, and a sinful nature. This negative view of us as human beings is a distortion of the biblical witness and what it means to be created in the image of God. This distorted perspective dominates many indi-viduals in our society, including in our churches, and can lead to problems of misuse, denials, abuse, destructive patterns, and failure to take responsibility for expressed feelings. When we are burdened or controlled by our feelings in negative and destructive ways, there is little vitality, joy, or feeling good.

This book will focus only on some selected feelings. Each chap-ter will feature a feeling: anxiety, doubt, anger, guilt, fatigue, fear, joy, peace, and wonder. The focus in the final chapter is on "the faith that counts" in life's journey. If these gifts by God's design are affirmed and expressed in negative ways and destructive behaviors or patterns, they can contribute to "disease" and our lack of wholeness and abundant living. These feelings are as troublesome for Christians as for non-Christians. They may be hidden or denied. If strong and persistent feelings are carried or expressed in negative ways or behav-ior patterns for any length of time, they can become *monsters*. The bigger the monsters become, the harder it is for them to be tamed and controlled to be of use. These monsters were called demons in Jesus's day. Our feelings and faith are companion gifts within us by God's design. Faith without feelings is restrictive and destructive in abundant living. Faith without failings is dead! It is not sound bibli-cal teaching and a fallacy to make any of these feelings a test of faith, including the presence or absence of doubt.

The Psalms reflect the emotional highs and lows of human exis-tence. Jesus, as the Living Word of God becoming flesh, expressed his feelings on many occasions during his life's journey, including, among others, anxiety, sorrow, grief, fatigue, anger, joy, wonder, and loneliness. In Jesus's life, feelings are seen as normal expressions in the human experience. We see here that with our gift of faith, we do not need to deny our feelings and the reality of our world as it is.

Journey with me through this book to experience inspiration, encouragement, support, and perhaps some healing as you affirm the gifts of feelings and faith for abundant living along your life's journey.

# Chapter 1

# *Live a Day at a Time with Anxiety*

*So don't worry about tomorrow, for tomorrow will bring its own worries. Today's trouble is enough for today.*

*—Matthew 6:34 (NLT)*

The first feeling we will consider is anxiety. In Matthew 6:25–34, Jesus teaches a lesson on anxiety. He uses the analogy of the lilies of the field and the birds of the air. When I read this scene, I recall my boyhood days on Grandpa Joe's grain and dairy farm in central Iowa. I would run through the alfalfa fields with my arms waving in the cool summer breeze. I would lie down in the alfalfa, gazing up at the barn swallows soaring freely in the clear blue sky against the fluffy clouds. This was a scene and world without anxiety, though I still had that gift within my being. However, in the same alfalfa field, I watched my Grandpa Joe get mauled to unconsciousness by a mean bull that he was bringing back to the barn. The bull was to be hauled off to market the next morning. As a seven-year-old, I watched in panic from the barn gate. These contrasting feelings happen to the same boy in the same Iowa barnyard.

I can identify very easily here with Ziggy, one of my favorite cartoon characters. Ziggy is staring off into space, head titling heavenward. He cries out, "It's hard to be human, ya know." Ziggy speaks for all of us. With limited control over what happens along our life's journey and over our tomorrows that so quickly become our todays, death then comes. It may be caused by a natural cause, an accident, or a disease. It may be caused by a pandemic, like COVID-19. This crisis has united the global human family with a common threat to life. It has united humanity in all the feelings that we share as common sisters and brothers created in God's image. Anxiety and fear, not only of the virus but of death itself, tops the list of feelings. Frustration, fatigue, anger, and doubts about when and what normal will return abound. The human existence is, at best, a challenge with interludes of fun and joy. At worst, it is hard, often unfair, and frequently filled with anxiety. We are frustrated by this reality. We are quite often anxious to the point of fear and being immobilized by anxiety.

So which of Jesus's teachings will apply to us today for such a feeling? Jesus tells the crowd gathered around him in his Sermon on the Mount that they ought not to be anxious. Jesus's admonition here certainly speaks to us. If I am "tuned into" many of the people I have met, taught, or served along my journey, then I believe anxiety is one of our dominant traits today, especially in this season as I am writing this book. We are heeding the advice to hunker down and only go out for emergency needs and groceries. We are told to wear a mask to avoid getting infected by the COVID-19 virus. But even before the COVID-19 pandemic, we have become an anxiety-ridden people in our society. This is evidenced by the increase in drug usage, child and relationship abuse, schools and street shootings, career failures, and bankruptcies. This is only a few anxiety-ridden and anxiety-producing scenarios in our society,

Anxiety has the same root meaning in Latin as anger or anguish, *angere*. The closest to our translation is "to choke" or to the feeling of being "pushed tightly together." Anxiety then is a deterrent, keeping us from our vision, our joys, our energy, and our affections. If not controlled or treated, it can constrict our faith. Yes, even on our faith and our trust in others, including our trust in God. It chokes our vitality and suffocates our positive actions. Anxiety can be expressed as anger at oneself for what one doesn't know, what one can't control, and what one can't do.

So what is anxiety? Almost any definition will include the word *fear*. Sometimes our anxieties are due to objectless fears. That is, we just do not know why we are anxious. It's sort of like being in a dark room with a mosquito or sitting on a dock at a favorite lakeside in the moonlight. You know that the mosquito is there, but you can't see it. There are anxieties that have to do with the fear of failure in a race, a contest, a work project, or in a relationship. There is the fear of being unmasked for who we are by someone, like the shadowy side of our personality. There is fear in the uncertain medical exam, in the outcome of the treatment, and in how many days we have left in life's journey. Anxiety is the name of the monster feeling here. These fears can stimulate negative and self-destructive anxiety and behavior.

There is a good kind of anxiety. We must not conclude outright that Jesus is condemning all anxiety as foolish and harmful. I think we all are aware of the fact that nothing very significant would ever be accomplished without the aid of anxiety. Students who aim high academically will be anxious. Parents who are paying for the high cost of education will also be anxious. Authors who take on the challenge of writing a book will have some anxieties along the publication process with editorial and deadline expectations to meet. The sheer stimulation of the anxiety is part of the incentive for the undertaking. The anxiety does for the long haul what caffeine does for the night before the final exams or the deadline for sending the final manuscript copy off to one's publisher.

Anxiety is not always good or bad. Potentially this gift by God's design in us is both. If I have been speeding and I spot a patrol car, a feeling of anxiety automatically comes over me. Slowing down is good. Slowing down means saving me from a $150 fine. Likewise, anxiety may take on the form of the exhilarating emotional response that overcomes us in times of danger. This certainly is not bad. It sometimes saves a life, like heeding the warning sign as one stands too close to the viewing edge at the Grand Canyon.

What kind of anxiety did Jesus have in mind? Jesus says here that anxiety is destructive in our lives. We have anxiety when we do not let go of the past with all its burdens and mistakes. It is this anxiety—combined with the frustrations, worries, disappointments, and hurts of the present day—that can create anxious feelings and wonderment whether tomorrow will be worth living at all. It is that anxious fear that we carry daily from the past into today. Jesus has in mind here this anxious fear that we can and do often have. They are real or perceived fears that we carry into our todays and shouldered under all the uncertainties of our tomorrows. We can sum all of this with the doubt and fear of not being accepted in God's eternal family that awaits us. Indeed, the sign we see in Jesus's life is that by gift, blessing, and promise, we are all Easter people in this Good Friday kind of world. Much of the fear in this anxiety is false evidence. Thus, the resolution and peace we have here is in Jesus's words, "Be not anxious! It is God's good pleasure to give each of us a place in the kingdom." Jesus wants us to understand that the fear of tomorrow and weight of yesterday makes even the strongest to stumble in anxiety.

Some of us need to give ourselves a good talking-to here. We need to stand ourselves up before a mirror. We need to say quite bluntly, "Now see here, the past is gone! Utterly and irretrievably gone! The burning is burnt! I am now one of God's beloved daughters, one of God's beloved sons. I always have been by image design and in the good news in Jesus." Be not anxious. It is God's good will and joy to give us this eternal identity and home. Then if to live a day at a time means that we must stop living in the past, it also must mean that we need to stop living in fear of the future. We are free to make the most of the present day. Each day is new for the rest of life's journey until we live forever free in God's renewed creation. Remember again what Jesus tells us in this scene, "Never be troubled over tomorrow for tomorrow will take care of itself. The day's own trouble is enough for the day" (Matt. 6:34).

I have a morning prayer mantra on a glass paperweight on my bedside stand. It reminds me each new morning of Jesus's admonition. I recite it to myself several times throughout the new day, "Lord, help me to remember that nothing will happen to me today that you and I can't handle together." The best way we can lessen tomorrow's anxieties and burdens is by making the most of living life each day. Jesus wants us to see that all life is organized by God on the principle of "a day at a time." We all are aware that victory in anything hangs on a series of victories, which we must win one by one. In any sport, the victory is won by one play, one hit, one basket, one jump, or one step at a time. I certainly had this lesson reinforced in the sports I played years ago, but not without some anxiety as the championship goals were sought and often won. We know from life's experience that a courtship is built on one meaningful date after another. A marriage grows and sustains itself one fulfilling day at a time. A book takes shape for publication and is read one word, one sentence, and one page at a time.

As far as living life's journey successfully in our contemporary society, Jesus is not talking against our making plans for the day, the month, or a career. Jesus is not talking against life insurance, preventive medicine, or savings accounts for our children's college education and IRA's for our retirement years. He is not talking against our learning, our being treated, our being healed, our being guided by doctors, counselors, life coaches, and spiritual directors. These caregivers can and do help us to see, to name, to resolve, and to dump our anxieties and fears.

For more than a decade, while on the staff of a National Lutheran Church, I facilitated spirituality retreats at retreat centers across the States. As a naming, resolving, and healing exercise, I would ask participants to write their monster anxieties and fears on a rock with a marker. To be freed, they would toss the rocks into the lake, remembering their baptismal washing—"Washed clean! Behold, I am new!"—or I would have them journal an anxiety situation or make a list of fears. In this exercise, what was buried alive in the basement of their conscious self could be privately brought up. It could be let go as we burned their journaling in the evening bonfire. There are things and actions we can take to be freed and healed from our negative anxieties or fears. An annual physical should be on our self-care list. We should take responsibility for our life's journey and our circumstances along the way. Jesus is simply saying that we are not to be anxious, burdened, and fearful about tomorrow. We must not expend all our emotional resources—mind, body, and spirit—by bearing tomorrow's anticipated needs, failures, rejections or problems in advance before they happen. Again, be reminded that many of these projected fears are "false evidence appearing real." This can become the trap Jesus wants to liberate us from. Jesus is speaking about the destructive habit of anticipating conditions, troubles, and tragedies. Most of these never actually take place. They are more conquerable than we make them out to be.

Then is anxiety the enemy of faith or is it the very condition given to us from being created in the image of God? In Martin Luther's catechism, we are taught that the first gift of the Spirit is faith. This gift is to be recognized, experienced, affirmed, and expressed through good and fruitful daily acts. When we recognize and affirm this gift, we are recognizing God's presence and grace in us. Faith and fear are not independent or exclusive of one another. They are companions within us on the stages of life's journey. That is, if you have one, you do not eliminate the other. God's presence, gifts, and grace upon us does not nullify our natures. We are free to make choices. We are free to act, potentially for the good. With our freedom, by choice or in ignorance, we can and do act for the bad. God's presence and grace, which works faith in us, does not magically eliminate our human failures. God's presence and grace absolves, frees, and empowers us for abundant living along life's journey. We are not to be captivated by our anxieties or fears along the way or by our fear of being eternally rejected for our projected anxieties and fears. God's presence and grace give us the strength of faith to both affirm and use our anxiety as a gift and stop them from being destructive in our relationships, work, and activities. Living in and with our faith gift, we are given the power and the freedom to rise above these anxieties and fears that are negative and destructive. In this faith, the first gift of the Spirit present and active in and through us, we also possess what we need to face the anxiety at our journey's end. We need not fear that moment. We are by sign and promise in Jesus—"Easter-people in a Good Friday kind of world!" We need not fear tomorrow if we live one day at a time in the light of Jesus's way and promises.

From my experience, a surprising number of Christians are among those who have a hard time with faith. This is linked, I believe, to their lack of trust in God's promise of forgiveness or it is often linked to broken and low self-esteem. This is especially true if they have made a mess in their lives. We can have a hard time living in God's grace that forgives all our past, good and bad, and live daily with less anxiety by living forgivingly first toward ourselves and then towards others.

The past is past. It has been cleared through God's grace, white as fresh fallen snow or as bright as your computer screen after hitting the delete button! It is this truth and reality that Jesus had in mind for the good news along our life's journey and acceptance of our inevitable end. This is why Jesus said not to be anxious about tomorrow. If God promises to care for the lilies of the fields and the birds of the sky, will he not provide for our tomorrow, we who are created in God's image? Mulling over our mistakes of yesterday paralyzes the efforts of today. Excessive regret over bad acts and past blunders, unable to forgive ourselves or others, only hides our mistakes deep inside us, causing anxieties. In turn, this causes constriction of our spirit of life, vitality, joy and even our gift of faith. It suffocates our energies for joyful, radiant, and productive living one day at a time.

In simple faith and surest trust, we are to commit our uncertain future to God. Let us leave our future to God. Let us trust it to God's power, creativity, and grace. Since we always stand in love and grace before God, we need not fear an unknown future, especially, since a life's journey in this Creation has already been awesome. There is a hymn verse that speaks so clearly to this anxiety:

> Said the robin to the sparrow,
> "I should really like to know,
> Why those anxious human beings
> Rush about and worry so."
> Said the sparrow to the robin,
> "Friend, I think that it must be,
> That they have no Heavenly Father,
> Such as cares for you and me!" (Elizabeth Cheney)

Faith can keep company with our God-given set of feelings, including *anxiety*. These feelings can be dealt with and lived with, but never denied or removed. We are not asked by Jesus to live an unreal life, a denial of the very One in whose image we are created. Jesus is teaching us in this scene and others not to make the denial of our feelings, including anxiety, a test or condition of faith being present. If we recognize and affirm our gift of faith along life's journey as God's active presence in us, we too can *live one day at a time*!

## The Journey Verse

Rejoice in the Lord always; again I will say, rejoice. Let your reasonableness be known to everyone. The Lord is at hand; do not be anxious about anything, but in everything by prayer and supplication with thanksgiving let your requests be made known to God. And the peace of God, which surpasses all understanding, will guard your hearts and your minds in Christ Jesus.

(Phil. 4:4–7 ESV)

# Chapter 2

# *The Good in Honest Doubt*

*Now the eleven disciples went to Galilee, to the mountain to which Jesus had directed them. And when they saw him they worshiped him, but some doubted.*

—Matthew 28:16–17 (ESV)

In chapter 1 on anxiety, we observed how Jesus, being God in the flesh, expressed his feelings on many occasions. In Jesus's life, we see our feelings as normal expressions. Jesus's feelings, as with our own, often arose in his encounter, involvement, and response to the circumstances of others. Like the Son of God, we have our set of feelings as daughters and sons created by design in God's image. Jesus's set of or expressed feelings were always his own in these encounters, as our feelings are recognized and affirmed as our own. Just as Jesus is responsible for his feelings, we are solely responsible for ours. Our set of feelings were also declared as good by God in the opening chapter of Genesis. "Then God saw everything that He had made, and indeed *it was* very good" (Gen. 1:31 NKJV). Our feelings do not belong only to our fallen or broken natures.

Jesus grieved the death of his friend, Lazarus. Embracing the situation and reality, he wept. We should remember this affirmation of honest doubt as we encounter and wrestle with some sad, tragic, or disappointing experiences along our life's journey. There were times when Jesus looked with anger at the hard hearts of the Pharisees.

Jesus extended compassion to the widow of Nain whose only son had died. Jesus spoke of his loneliness and anxiety near the end of his teaching and healing ministry. Jesus prayed alone all night in the darkness of the garden of Gethsemane while his closest disciples kept falling asleep.

In Jesus's likeness, we are creatures of feelings. God's love for us does not depend on our highs and lows, our successes or failures. God keeps no scorecard on us. As people created in God's image, we have a complex emotional makeup. One of our feelings is *doubt*. In this chapter, we will take a look at the feeling of doubt. Like our other feelings, doubt can be both good and bad. Doubt needs to be understood and handled. It should not be denied or suppressed. It should not be taught or judged as a sign of a weak faith or lack of faith. The gift is there for life's journey. Faith is a gift of the Spirit within us to be recognized, affirmed, and expressed. We may choose not to do so. We may choose not to recognize it, claim it, and express it openly, faithfully, and boldly. Doubt is not a feeling that is ever totally absent in faith. We can stop beating ourselves down for honest doubting.

What is doubt? For starters, I like to say that doubt is the friction caused by a great truth passing through our limited or fixed mindset. It is the upsetting friction caused by an encounter or challenge beyond our current abilities, understanding, or resources, such as the COVID-19 pandemic. It may be aroused daily in the battle against cancer and the painful, nauseating effects of the chemo treatments. The fear in this long battle arouses doubts as possible outcomes are faced, not the least being the threat of one's life journey ending. Doubt is the friction caused in our minds by a frightening challenge, an unbelievable experience, or a new insight that breaks open our fixed knowledge box or belief system. Doubts may be caused by the surprising reality in the twenty-first century. It took centuries to accept and to adjust to the idea that our world is only a speck in a universe of universes and the reality that the Earth is not flat nor the center of the one universe.

Honest doubt may be the friction caused in one's thinking or one's faith affirmation at the new reality of life that the women experienced at Jesus's tomb. On that first Easter morning, Mary Magdalene, Mary the mother of James, and Salome were shocked with honest doubt when they found the boulder was rolled away. The tomb was opened and exposed to the bright sunlight. Only the burial shrouds were found in the tomb where Jesus had been laid. In Mark 16, we have an eyewitness's account of Jesus's resurrection. The women entered the tomb and were alarmed. A young man standing there said to them, "Do not be alarmed. You are looking for Jesus of Nazareth, who was crucified. He has been raised; he is not here... Go tell his disciples and Peter that he is going ahead of you to Galilee; there you will see him, just as he told you" (Mark 16:6–7). The account tells us that they told no one at first for they were so afraid and full of honest doubt. They were prepared by Jesus for this day, this experience, and this new reality. Only the feeling of honest doubt could undergird their faith. Mary Magdalene went out and told the disciples that Jesus was alive. At first, they would not believe it (Mark 16:11). There lives more faith in honest doubt!

Near the end of Matthew's gospel, we read another account of the post-resurrection appearances of Jesus. In chapter 28, there is this interesting scene, "Then the eleven disciples went to Galilee, to the mountain where Jesus had told them to go. When they saw Jesus, they worshiped him; but some doubted" (Matt. 28:16–17 NIV). Does the honesty in the disciples' encounter with Jesus in this scene surprise you? Does the story raise any doubts in your mind? Remember that Jesus told his disciples that he would meet them again after his crucifixion and death. These events were a part of the very purpose and mission of his life's journey in this world. This meeting with Jesus was to move all of them beyond honest doubt, including denying Peter and doubting Thomas.

Is it strange to you that they doubted their teacher and journey friend? I can easily identify with them. There is a mix of Peter and Thomas in me. I know I have denied Jesus's way in some thoughts, choices, and acts. Yes, Thomas is also in me. I am a doubter, a seeker for new insights and the truth. Strange that they should have doubted Jesus...or is it? Jesus had been crucified. They were there hiding in the crowd in shock, horror, and honest doubt that this cruel scene was happening to their teacher. Some of them had seen it all. Jesus was with them again, even walking along the road to Emmaus (Luke 24:13–35) and talking with a couple of them about the events of the past week in Jerusalem. Later that week, Jesus gathered his doubting disciples for his last meal. Some needed to see the scars on his hands from the nails and the scars from the crown of thorns on his head, even touch the wound in his side from the spear to help them deal with their honest doubt. Jesus was indeed alive and with them again in their real world. Indeed there is more faith in honest doubt!

I wonder if they doubted their own senses, their own characters, their commitments, their promises, their loyalties, their memories from past lessons, and their faith itself. Yes, even their faith. Does any of this spark your doubts? Where is your honesty? The doubts in the women at the empty tomb and in the disciples with the risen Jesus did not prevent them from talking to, eating with, and worshiping Jesus with amazement and joy. In fact, it most likely encouraged them to affirm their faith. Doubt certainly made them touch the scars and watch closely to see how this Jesus broke his bread. They knew his usual manner from many meals together. They saw the bloodied Jesus taken down from the cross and laid in a secured tomb.

As the disciples and a group of women followers spent days with Jesus, he became more real to them. Their honest doubt resolved into affirming faith and spreading the good news in Jerusalem, Judea, and throughout the rest of their known world. Their faith grew. Their doubts fell into perspective. Jesus charged them to go and tell the world all what he had taught them and all that he had done for their new and forever life. Jesus promised them that as he had risen to new life, so shall all of God's daughters and sons rise anew in his likeness.

Doubt has its contribution in some of our experiences along our journey days. Both conscientious people and faith-filled people—that is, all those who recognize and affirm this God-given gift within themselves—can worry over their doubts more than is needful or helpful. There are, however, those situations when doubt is indispensable. Doubt warns us when the vehicle we are driving is no longer up to the standards of safety. Perhaps we need a new set of brakes or a new set of tires to avoid that possible blowout. I remember an experience years ago with my son Kent's first car, an old Peugeot. We wondered why the steering wheel vibrated so much between 30 and 45 miles per hour. We knew why after the right front tire blew out. We knew the tires were mounted unevenly, but we could not see the bulge that was apparently on the inner side of the tire. There was no shaking after the new tires were put on.

Doubt may warn a painter from the dangers of a wobbly ladder. Doubt at the Kennedy Space Center during a countdown might delay a rocket launch. The delay, however, might save the lives of the astronauts in the space capsule and millions of our tax dollars. Likewise, doubts may periodically X-ray the bones of contentions in our relationships. Our missed expectations, fears, or problems can be scrutinized before they have any impact on us. Doubt also warn us before the weight of life's problems breaks us down. Be attentive to your doubts.

It is good for us to remember that Jesus did not condemn or reject the honest doubter, a person who is struggling with a circumstance in his or her life and searching for truth, respect, acceptance, or a healing. I am grateful for the support and doubts in my own life. From a Nicodemus, the woman at Jacob's well, or the distraught father who asked Jesus to heal his epileptic son, we see in these situations that dim hope, for any reason, is an expression of honest doubt and faith.

Faith and doubt play hide and seek in our hearts at times. It did for the disciples. Perhaps that is what we are to see in Jesus's all-night prayer struggle in Gethsemane (Mark 14:32–42)? Before rising to face his betrayer and those standing at the garden entrance to arrest him, we hear honest doubt in Jesus's prayer from his struggling heart. "If possible, can this event pass from me?" was Jesus's plea. "Father, not what I want, but what you want." What happened here is as true for Jesus as it is potentially true for us. More faith lives in honest doubt. There may be those among us who claim to have no doubts. Most of us have known and continue to experience the inner struggles revealed in the disciples, in the women followers, and in Jesus himself. We, too, can pray, "Lord, I believe. Help me, Lord, in my unbelief. Help my doubtful heart!"

Let us now shift our concern to the question, if we are to conquer doubt, how shall we go about it? The first thing we can do is not berate or condemn ourselves for having doubts! We cannot force ourselves to believe. Faith is a gift of the Spirit within us. We can become aware of that gift as we can of our feeling gifts. Over time, we can grow in our awareness, understanding, affirmation, and expressions of that gift of faith. We may choose to develop a belief system. It often takes the shape of a body of doctrines that bears a brand label. Our faith and personal belief system are not one and the same. Many of our doubts can be caused by this confusion and fallacy.

Faith is God's gift to us. It is manifested by the Spirit's working within us. It is not to be judged as "more or less" or as "strong or weak." We can, however, question our faith and the source of our doubts. Left unchecked and not resolved in positive ways, we can hate our skepticism. If we journey too long and too far down our personal Gethsemane, we can hate ourselves or even hate God. We can declare that God is dead. We can declare that there is no God. The gift is still there in the wellspring of our being.

There are those today who seek to deny and repress their doubts. They do this because they think it is a weakness to reveal, admit, or talk about their doubts. Many young people leave the nurturing and supportive teaching of their family and their congregation to venture off into life's journey with the assumption that it is wrong for Christians to doubt. Such youth tend to judge others as having too weak of a faith. They tend to be hypocritical. It is unfortunate when this is the teaching in any congregation or family. Honest questioning throughout our lifelong journey, wherever it may lead, is a central part of what it means to love the Lord with all our minds. Such honest doubting leads finally to a healthy maturity and to peace of mind in the awareness that Jesus has a hold on us for eternity through his lived-out obedience, love, death, and resurrection for us. Jesus's life is God's grace on all of us. We do not have a hold on Jesus because of our wisdom, our boxed answers that are more informed with the best theology or philosophy. We do not have a grip on Jesus by our own certainty. Such means of being saved with no openness for honest doubting are idolatries.

Thank God that one of Jesus's prayers on the cross for all humanity was, "Father, forgive all of them, especially those who do not know what they are saying or doing!" This affirmation and inclusive blessing were also acted out by Jesus at his Last Supper in an upper room in Jerusalem. Jesus gave the bread and passed the cup to all gathered with him, including betraying Judas, denying Peter, and doubting Thomas. The disciples gathered with each their own baggage of gifts expressed daily in good and bad ways. They were promised to be so blessed and renewed every day as they lived in Jesus's way and fulfilled his mission in the world. What a sign to remember as we live out our journey.

The second thing we can do to affirm our gift of doubt, including our honest doubting, is to remind ourselves frequently that faith is not an intellectual certainty. It is not an accomplishment on our part by which we are approved and finally blessed as daughters and sons in God's family. It is not something proven by sight or by volumes of books. When Mary met Jesus in the garden on Easter morning, Jesus said to her, "Touch me not!" When doubting Thomas met Jesus a week later, Jesus stretched forth his hands to silence Thomas's doubt and all the doubters in the generations to follow. Jesus then said, "Have you believed because you have seen me? More blessed are those who have not seen me and yet believe in me" (John 20:29). The third thing we can do is recognize and affirm that we don't achieve faith or manifest faith without openly and honestly exercising our God-given gift and capacity to doubt. Not to do so is to deny being created in God's image. It is to oversimplify who we are as human beings. Such a security is false. It is religious idolatry. It is grounded more in fear than in faith. It is not faith at all. It is self-security in closed boxes of taught understanding and false contentment.

There is at least one more awareness and practice that can be helpful in our affirming and controlling this doubt gift. To repress or deny them is to mishandle them. There is another way, exemplified by the disciples and the father who brought his epileptic son to Jesus to be healed. Be honest with your doubts. Acknowledge them. Share them. Confess them. Talk them out for freeing resolution with a trusted friend, counselor, or spiritual director. Seek to grow in wisdom, and in stature, and in favor before God and others as Jesus did through his life's journey. What feeling was at work in Jesus when he asked in the wilderness, "Who am I? What am I to accomplish? How am I to do it?" What feeling was at work when Jesus pleaded in Gethsemane for some other way than the cross? What feeling was at work when Jesus cried out, "My God, my God, why have you forsaken me?" Perhaps some honest doubting?

Doubt's purpose or doubt's grace in our lives is to make room for safety; for understanding to emerge; and for the work of the Spirit to influence, guide, transform, and heal us. Doubt's purpose then is for abiding faith to be affirmed and expressed openly in our doubting as the Spirit works in and with us in all our needs and situations. To understand Jesus's way of handling doubt, we need to appreciate the ministry of doubt in the life of faith. In the likeness of Jesus's life pattern, take your doubts to God in prayer. Let us then get it into our minds that there is nothing wrong with us when we have doubts. Honest doubt, freely acknowledged and expressed, is not wrong or a weakness. It is a heathier behavior for us than a gnawing pain in the soul or affirming a false sense of security in one's absolutes.

There is a dangerous side to doubt, however. It is possible, when doubt runs wild, that it ends up in the emptiness of despair. Because of this danger, doubt as a feeling must be watched and controlled. Doubt is potentially a more severe source of personal crisis and destructive behavior than other feelings we might be struggling with. It has been said, "To doubt at the top of the head while believing with the bottom of the heart is good and often fruitful. But to doubt at the bottom of the heart while believing only at the top of the head is disastrous." When doubt has weakened life at its foundations, there is despair because it is possible for God to be denied and for the very meaning of life itself to be at stake.

Doubt is a feeling to be understood. It must be controlled, like all of our feelings. Apostle Paul reminds us of this responsibility in his list of the fruits of the Spirit in us in his pastoral letter to the Galatians. The fruit of the Spirit is love, joy, peace, patience, kindness, generosity, faithfulness, gentleness, and self-control (Gal. 5:22). Doubt is a shadow companion of faith in God's gifts for our life's journey. By doubting, the Spirit can and does work to lead us into fuller truth, abundant living, and, ultimately to our new forever life with the risen Jesus. Our inheritance gift is not dependent on our feelings or our "belief box". We are free indeed! We are free to doubt openly and honestly. Our inheritance is dependent only on God's will, choice, and love for us through Jesus. Let the faith within our hearts freely and boldly affirm daily, and in our last breath, "Yes, Lord, I believe! Lord, help me in my doubting!"

## The Journey Verse

I lift my eyes to the hills. From where will my help come from? My help comes from the Lord, who made heaven and earth. He will not let your foot be moved; he who keeps you will not slumber... The Lord is your keeper; the Lord is your shade at your right hand... The Lord will keep you from all evil, he will keep your life. The Lord will keep your going out and your coming in from this time on and forevermore.

(Psalm 121:1–3, 5, 7–8 ESV)

# Chapter 3

# *The Right in Honest Anger*

*In the temple courts [Jesus] found people selling cattle, sheep and doves, and the money changers sitting at their tables exchanging money. So he made a whip of cords, and drove all from the temple courts, both sheep and the cattle; he scattered the coins of the money changers and overturned their tables. To those who sold doves, he said, "Get these out of here! Stop turning my Father's house into a market."*
—John 2:14–16 (NIV)

We continue our reflections on selected feelings as inherent gifts in God's design of us. In this chapter, we will reflect on anger. We have all expressed anger and experienced anger. We have all experienced destructive things from the actions of angry people. If we are honest with ourselves, we have felt and seen the damage our expressed anger caused on others. Sometimes to people who are close and dear to us.

Jesus taught us a central principle for abundant living. We are to love God and one another as God has shown it through Jesus. We are to love even our enemies and those we do not like. Somehow this teaching can cause us confusion, denial, or suppression of this gift. We may even think that it is wrong to get angry. Yet this anger has a home within us. It had a home within Jesus. In this chapter, we will reflect on some scenes where Jesus expressed anger. Yes, anger is even seen and acted out in daily situations in the life of "the Word become flesh," in the life of Jesus of Nazareth.

Anger is a natural gift by God's design. This feeling seldom erupts at the boiling point. We hiss and snarl, argue and swear. We give someone "the finger" or they give it to us! We glare at people, roll our eyes, or give the silent treatment. In places of employment, we belittle work associates and sabotage bosses. Sometimes we even return with a gun after not getting the promotion we thought we earned or after being fired. Such encounters are happening more frequently, as reported in the evening news. We watch our favorite TV judge or talk show host try to maintain some civility as separating couples, parents, children, estranged neighbors battle it out over issues and disputes. What are we expressing here? What are we doing in these actions? Are we justified in these behaviors? Are we honestly angry?

Our feelings, including anger, are a part of our birth package by God's design and intent. They are the tools in our toolbox for effective and abundant living and for handling our frustrations, disappointments, hurts, and fears. From birth to about two years old, we experience our world through feelings. Once we gain our self-awareness and we can use words, we can begin to name our expressed feelings. Those feelings, which are natural and subjective, become known and objective, even if not always controlled and expressed in good ways. Out of frustration, a two-year-old will bite or hit you if you don't give in to what he or she wants. Such acts is one of the first signals of the basic human feeling of anger. Parents need to teach young children how to affirm these feelings and use them appropriately for their good and the good of others.

Anger has a purpose. At worst, it is a natural gift gone bad. Used properly, anger can be helpful. Most outbursts do not result in violence or in aggressive behavior, but improves behavior or understanding in a relationship. We will see in our reflections on Jesus way of living and interacting with individuals or with a crowd in situations, that anger was designed as an emergency response. As a natural gift, anger is not meant to be used and expressed constantly and intensely, like pressing one's foot on the gas pedal. This is like when we are driving our car. It is not wise or good to have one's foot to heavy on the gas pedal and certainly seldom to the floorboard.

Each person needs to learn that anger, carefully handled and honestly expressed, can be an effective "grace tool." It can be used to cope with life's threats in releasing hurts and in talking out openly and honestly difficult issues and situations. That is, anger can work for good. Expressed anger can work for understanding, resolution, and healing within oneself and within relationships. This is equally true for children and the youth. How many parent and child relationships become abusive and destructive? How many early friendships or marriages were hurt and lost because this *grace tool* was not used properly in the situations? There are times for all of us when we reach our limit, the absolute limit, of our patience.

The young child can say no with the feeling we name anger. In fact, if the child's spirit is not broken by negative conditioning about expressing anger, a child will express anger automatically. Hopefully, this healthy expression will not happen uncontrollably too often. When a child is taught to express no anger, that child will mature into adulthood with a pattern of being deceitfully nice. This behavior can be very manipulative, oppressive, and abusive. It is a given that from early childhood, we never cease to experience life and other people apart from our feelings. We shift our inner gears, our inner gifts, into the feelings we express. Those who expect us to never get too angry are asking the impossible. They are asking us, in fact, to deny our nature created in the likeness of God, the very God we see present in Jesus. Yes, anger is one of God's emotions. Anger itself is not sin, but anger can be expressed sinfully. God created human beings with the capacity to experience and express anger as an emotional physical action in some chosen circumstances. Anger can lead to positive ways, an appropriate or justifiable behavior or action.

COVID-19 turned our world upside down, globally and locally. The battle against this new life-threatening virus quickly became a global war uniting allies and foes against a common enemy. This new unity was evident in the compassionate service of doctors and nurses, first responders, and support staff. Knowledge about this new global virus and resources like ventilators, testing swabs, masks, disease immunity specialists, and medical personnel were shared across state and national borders. The COVID-19 virus was no respecter of race, color, gender, or creed. It was a threat to young and old alike, attacking everyone from infants to those in their golden years. State executive orders and directives shut down corporations and businesses from the super giants down to the family bakery. Manufacturing facilities, stores, super malls, restaurants, bars, sports arenas, baseball stadiums, beaches, and parks were all shut down. All schools, public and private, first closed for two months and then for the remainder of the school year. Parents became teachers as their children continued their class lessons and projects via their laptops and tablets, guided by their schoolteachers. Worship centers of all faith expressions were closed for months into the summer and fall. Nothing continued in whatever had been normal routine in daily life.

The COVID-19 virus apparently started in China in late 2019. Cases surfaced in northern Italy and quickly spread south, killing thousands. It surfaced in France and Spain and spread to more than a hundred nations in the first quarter of 2020. By early March, Seattle and New York City became hot spots. Thousands upon thousands of cases overwhelmed hospitals, exhausting resources and their compassionate, caring staffs. At great risks to their lives, they worked extended shifts in heroic efforts to save lives. In spite of their heroic efforts and constant compassionate caregiving, deaths skyrocketed daily beyond morgue capacities. The shortages in essential testing supplies, ventilators, masks, and hospital staff soon caused frustration and exhaustion as dedicated staff and volunteers risked their own lives to flight this battle against COVID-19. Our federal government's response was late and inadequate, at best. By May, more than three million known coronavirus cases were recorded worldwide. More than a million known cases were recorded and treated in the United States with the epicenters in the New York, New Jersey, Washington, and California regions. The death toll surpassed sixty thousand throughout the States. In most situations, family and friends were not allowed to enter hospitals and care centers to touch, hug, and say their goodbyes to their spouses, children, and friends killed by COVID-19. By mid-September, the COVID-19 numbers reached a soaring six and a half million cases and more than one hundred and ninety-five thousand deaths of all ages, genders, and races in the United States. The numbers reached over two hundred and eight thousand cases and over five thousand deaths in Arizona, where I was in lockdown at the time of writing this book.

The national shutdown in the United States caused unemployment to rise by late April to a record-topping over 27.5 million, leaving millions without a paycheck or saving funds to pay off their monthly mortgage or rent, buy food, and pay bills. The billions of dollars of federal relief refunds for households and businesses was slow and late in getting to the local situations of dire need. What was so amazing to see in the first months of this battle against a common life-threatening enemy was the numerous signs and reported stories of unity, compassion, empathy, sharing, and self-giving risks of life itself. Patience endured! Anger was contained within and generally controlled. Frustrations, stress, and despair were mounting. The strict guidelines for home confinement, social distancing, and wearing a protective face mask while getting groceries and essential meds or walking your dog for exercise soon tested people's patience. Needing a paycheck for mortgage, rent, monthly bills, and essentials; getting back on the golf course or the beach; or getting to a favorite bar, restaurant, or baseball game soon give rise to record-setting 911 calls for domestic abuse.

Street protests in major cities across the country began to increase in the number of occurrences and size of the crowds. Some protesters even showed up with their large guns, waving signs that the shutdown was a violation of their Constitution rights. The intensity of the emotions increased. Anger was expressed in the shouting crowds and on the signs they carried. The anger intensified as the shutdown, home confinement, and social distancing directives were extended through May and into June in most states. These demonstrations were good for the expression of feelings, concerns, and issues. They are and were positive outlets for anger. However, as the emotions intensified, the anger in some demonstrations turned bad. In many cities, justified anger turned to violence and some shootings.

The Bible mentions no emotion more often than anger. There are more than 275 references to this basic human feeling. This does not include such related feelings as wrath or fury. I like to call these feelings heated-up anger. There are no biblical commands to repress or deny anger. There are examples of when and how to express anger, such as Jesus's angry acts in the entrance to the temple when he drove out the money changers and merchants selling animals for offerings. There are admonitions to curb anger. We see in the Scriptures that anger is bad, a sin when used without just cause. The people who believed in God throughout the centuries of the first covenant acknowledged the Lord's anger. They did so even if they did not always respect it or respond with changed and good behavior. A few selected verses can help us see this perspective:

- Numbers 14:18 says, "The Lord is slow to anger."
- Psalm 6:1 states, "O Lord, rebuke me not in your anger."
- Psalm 145:8 notes, "The Lord is gracious and merciful, slow to anger and abounding in steadfast love."

In both Luke 19:36–48 and John 2:13–22, we have Jesus, as the embodiment and presence of God, entering the outer courtyard entrance to the Jerusalem temple. Seeing the crooked moneychangers peddling their goods and selling animals for offerings, Jesus drove them out of the temple in anger. Can you see Jesus kicking the tables over? Can you see him telling the moneychangers in disgust, "You robbers! You have turned this house of prayer into a den of thievery!"

All people become angry. We get angry at ourselves for foolish mistakes or costly misjudgments. We get angry at others for slighting us or for abusive words and behavior. We get angry at our children for not listening, for not following directions, for not being just like the persons we imaged or want them to be. Such expressions of anger can be abusive. They can be a violation of a child's spirituality. We get angry at God for not seeming to be more real to us; for not being more supportive; and for not healing us quickly or giving relief from chronic pain for ourselves, a loved one, spouse, family member, a special friend, or work associate. We especially get angry at God for not answering our prayers the way we want them answered and on our timeline.

We each express anger differently. We do so according to our personalities. We do so according to how we have been taught and conditioned in our nurturing and educational settings, in our family, in our faith community, in society, and where we live. We do so according to how we choose to express our love, our openness, and our honesty toward others. Some will explode, others will simmer, and many will pray harder. Such prayers are common pleas for others to change without honestly looking at oneself to see and affirm what change might be necessary in oneself. Some will stop praying altogether, denying God. Others will kick themselves until there is not much love and confidence left for interacting with others in healthy ways.

If you believe that all anger is sinful and bad, that only God has a right to be angry, you probably attempt to conceal your anger frequently. You might even succeed in convincing yourself, while withdrawing and isolating yourself from others, that you never get angry. These efforts and self-delusions are not healthy. They can lead to personality disorders as well as emotional and physical health problems. That behavior pattern will be far more harmful than the anger itself.

Our anger can be properly and timely expressed, like Jesus did in the cleansing of the entrance to the Jerusalem temple. It can be controlled. It can be released and redirected in positive ways. This may involve talking out a concern or misunderstandings and taking the time to walk, exercise on a treadmill, or do meditation or yoga exercises. This self-care is to affirm anger as a natural gift. Denial is destructive to one's health, relationships, and productivity. Anger can never be made nonexistent. Anger can be repressed within yourself, but such behavior changes one's disposition. It will likely explode in harmful words or actions. People who talk about repressing anger are talking about the impossible. This teaching is a denial of what it means to be created in the image of God. Anger cannot be completely turned off for long periods of time without disastrous effects. A person will channel the anger within or release the anger toward others, directly or indirectly. When we try to turn off this natural feeling, we do not express our anger directly to the person or group we are at odds with or those who mistreat, threaten, or ignore us. What follows are the very destructive patterns of being deceitfully nice. Such anger is expressed in sarcasm, subtle remarks, hostile jokes, and the avoidance of the person or group. Such anger can be expressed indirectly in sloppiness or tardiness at school or at work. It can be masked by passive aggression or withholding affection.

How shall we define anger to help us get a handle on this feeling for our good? Anger is our emotional reaction to being misunderstood, threatened, or hurt. It is a normal reaction to experiencing a loss of a spouse, child, or friend as well as the loss of a significant relationship, a job promotion, or a property in a flood. Anger may be expressed due to being wronged, discriminated against, or abused by unjust rules. To describe anger, we often use common adjectives, such as hot-tempered, boiling mad, and short fuse. This does not mean that everyone should go around like a hothead in any of our relationships, marriages, and families and in places of work, schools, and recreation.

The affirmation of anger in the scriptures does not give us license to erupt at the slightest disappointment, frustration, or missed expectation. Anger will be expressed as we seek to speak our minds in love and self-control. When no anger is shown, perhaps there is not enough freedom, love, and trust to express the anger. When this is the situation, deceitfully nice expressions or indirect anger will be released. Given all this, it is no surprise that the scriptures offer many warnings for the expression of anger:

- "Whoever is slow to anger has great understanding, but he who has a hasty temper exalts folly." (Prov. 14:29).
- "A fool gives full vent to his anger, but a wise man quietly holds (throttles) it back." (Prov. 29:11 ESV).

A short outburst of anger, as I have described, is quite healthy in most instances. In most situations, we have a responsibility not to carry it further. I can remember an incident when somebody pulled out suddenly in a parking lot at a Dairy Queen, hitting my brand-new car. Did I get angry? I sure did! But that was the end of it. After I released a few chosen words, I got the man's phone number, address, and car insurance information. Such a natural involuntary release can help one gain conscious control over the situation.

Then there is a good use of anger. As troublesome as anger can be, the scriptures show examples of God's "righteous anger," expressed through the plagues, the warring nations, and the confrontation words of the prophets, Amos and Hosea. This *righteous anger* of God is continued through the "woe statements" of Jesus to the scribes and Pharisees:

> "Woe to you, scribes and Pharisees, hypocrites!
> For you tithe mint and dill and cumin, and have
> neglected the weightier matters of the law: justice
> and mercy and faithfulness… You blind guides,
> straining out the gnat and swallowing a camel."
> (Matt. 23:23–24 ESV)

Jesus used anger to protest injustice, religious and ethnic exclusiveness, lack of compassion and mercy, and inequality. In the light of Jesus's examples, anger is used as "faith active in love" when it protests selfishness, neglect, apathy, abuse, or hostility. Following his angry actions in the outer courtyard of the temple (John 2:13–22), Jesus claimed, "I am the temple!"

What is the purpose and meaning of Jesus being the real temple of God? As John writes in his first pastoral letter through the crucifixion and resurrection of Jesus, we have from God a sign, blessing, and promise, "Beloved, we are already sons and daughters of God" (1 John 3:2). Therefore, we live freely. We affirm, celebrate, and express who we are with our natural gifts and whose we are. Created in the image of the God, we see and know in Jesus. We are loved and redeemed through the life, death, and resurrection of Jesus, the true temple of God. Even though we have not and do not always express our natural feelings faithfully and in good ways, remember the promise in your daily journey: Beloved, we are already—always have been and always will be—sons and daughters of God! Jesus laid down his life on the cross for us. Jesus hovers over us in death and calls us forth to a forever life, risen in his likeness. Until then, Jesus is with us, in us, and for us as he is ahead of us. What a wonderful passion story for us and for our sisters and brothers, all created in the image of God with our package of feelings. What a wonderful promise! Each drop of Jesus's blood on the cross bought you and me not only a million years but a forever journey, without offering purchased oxen, sheep, or doves!

We are to daily affirm and express our anger freely, openly, honestly, and responsibly. As a grace tool, expressed anger opens the possibilities for resolutions and forgiveness. Anger, honestly expressed, is a part of abundant living in life's journey.

## The Journey Verse

"Be angry and do not sin; do not let the sun go down on your anger… Let all bitterness and wrath and anger and clamor and slander be put away from you, along with all malice. Be kind to one another, tenderhearted, forgiving one another, as God in Christ forgave you."

(Eph. 4:26, 31–32 ESV)

# Chapter 4

# The Hammering of Guilt

*Jesus said to her, "Everyone who drinks of this water will be thirsty again, but whoever drinks of the water that I will give them will never be thirsty. The water that I will give will become in them a spring of water welling up to eternal life." The woman said to him, "Sir, give me this water, so that I may not be thirsty or have to keep coming here to draw water."*
—John 4:13–15 (ESV)

The fourth feeling we shall discuss is guilt. This feeling has a twin named shame, which we will also discuss in this chapter. They are not one and the same, but shame is a close companion to guilt. Guilt and shame are two closely related, overlapping feelings. Where we find one, we almost always find the other, except in some persons with mental health conditions.

First, let us remind ourselves that our feelings—whatever they might be—are not bad by themselves. That is to say, our feelings are not sinful by themselves. They may point to our mistakes, our wrongdoings, or a wrong action done to us. Such wrong acts may be expressed toward God, oneself, or others. All of our varied feelings are a part of our birth package by design and intent as we each are created in God's image.

The double focus of guilt and shame confronts us with two related feelings we have for some experiences on life's journey. We, like the woman at Jacob's well, can be wasting away in our broken conditions, meaningless situations, or mistakes. We can be hammered by guilt for our acts or nonactions and likely by shame in some of those experiences. We can walk anew daily in the "living water" that Jesus gave the woman at Jacob's well and will give to us freely if we ask (John 4:7–30).

When we read, hear, or consider God's word of forgiveness and renewal, as taught and acted out by the Living Word, Jesus, we can be freed from the "hammering of guilt" and the "bondage of shame." As a daughter or a son of the Creator, we need this promise word and grace gift from the Messiah for our salvation. The psalmist says there is this groaning, this hammering within us, "When I kept silent *about my sin*, my body wasted away through my groaning all day long. For day and night Your hand was heavy upon me; my vitality was drained away as with the fever heat of summer" (Psalm 32:3–4 NASB). That is, there is this hammering within our inner selves. If we are honest and open enough to admit it to God and to each other, this groaning often drains us physically, emotionally, and spiritually. If denied too long, it can change or even destroy oneself and one's relationships. One can waste away in guilt and shame like a plant does under the scorching summer heat in a drought.

This can be illustrated by a story about a little girl who was preparing for a family trip to visit her grandmother. Her father was explaining to her why he could not go along. The father apologized to her, "I'm sorry that I can't go with you to visit grandmother, my dear. I have to stay home to work on my invoices." When the little girl arrived at her grandmother's house, she explained her daddy's absence this way, "Grandma, Daddy couldn't come! Daddy is having quite a bit of trouble with his conscience." I suppose some adult made up this story. Whatever its source, truth or fiction, the story describes a central problem for many people in our day of *meism* and *self-help*. Unlike the woman before Jesus at Jacob's well, the woman sitting there alone who did not deny her life's scenario sketched out by Jesus for her recognition and ownership, many people choose to live under the bondage of their illusions or the hammering of their denials. They have quite a bit of trouble with their consciences. They are plagued, sometimes defeated into despair by their guilt and their sense of shame.

There is a common saying, "A guilty conscience needs no accuser." I believe the takeaway is that guilt is a personal matter. Guilt is caused by our own acts or by the acts of our community or racial group. Guilt deals with what we should be doing or should not be doing. When we acknowledge it or say to ourselves, "I did a wrong act," it is an expression of guilt. If we say, "I hate myself" or "I am no good", it is an expression of shame. The feelings are related but not the same. Guilt has its source in the deficiency that is in our wrong, destructive acts. Shame has its source in a deficiency felt within oneself. We are often made victims of false guilt by the demands, standards, expectations, or judgments of others. This commonly happens when someone or a group insists that everyone should think, feel, and act like they do. The instigator is usually as guilty of wrong acts and of not measuring up.

What happens under this hammering of guilt and bondage of shame? The impulse is to hide and escape. If not dealt with, the end result is doubting one's own thoughts, which leads to doubting Jesus's teachings and promises. To repress one's own feelings leads to concealing one's own responsibility for acts and any shame associated with them, like the woman at Jacob's well did before Jesus. When we do this, we fail to ask Jesus in our thoughts and prayers, "Lord, give me a drink of your living water." Such a request takes affirmation of faith. To acknowledge and ask is to expose one's real self to the stinging pain of shame for how one has acted. Like the broken woman at Jacob's well, we feel shame because we tell our inner selves that we are never quite good enough to be accepted and to belong. This was the woman's feeling at Jacob's well. This woman had to draw water alone at midday rather than early in the morning with the other women. Shame isolates since shame starts in our relationships by wrong, harmful, and destructive acts. She knew she was guilty. She felt ashamed in her loneliness. The woman at Jacob's well says to Jesus, "How is it that you, a Jew, ask a drink of me, a woman of Samaria?" By birth, by life's situation and acts, and by life's relationships, apart from Jesus's acceptance as the Living Water, this woman no longer belonged even in her community. She lived daily under the hammering of guilt and the bondage of shame.

Guilt results when we commit a mistake or do a forbidden deed. Guilt results when we chose not to act as needed or do the right thing. We all fail at this. We accuse ourselves of doing or saying something wrong when the judges around us, correctly or wrongly, tell us we have erred. Guilt deals with what we do. We may not recognize or accept this truth in our behavior. In this denial, we bury alive our feelings of shame, like the woman at Jacob's well. We may choose or be forced to isolate ourselves until we are open, honest, and freed for resolution and healing. Having failed to live perfectly, whatever we have been taught or told, is the expected way. Whatever we understand is good and right living, we experience the hammering of guilt almost daily. If guilt is not faced and removed, we experience the hardening of our hearts and emotions. We experience self-reproach. Then we don't like and accept ourselves because of what we think, say, and do. This feeling, as an untamed monster in our lives, makes it harder for us to live and accept others, even those closest to us.

Guilt is caused by various kinds of actions. Some things that bother me may not bother you. For example, I usually feel guilty about wasting time. It is hard for me to watch TV very long without feeling uncomfortable. Guilt probably stems from being conditioned by the work ethics I was taught during my boyhood years in the corn belt and piety of central Iowa. I feel guilty that my time is slipping away without doing something constructive. Other people can feel quite at ease watching TV for hours, not to mention the quality of the programs they watch. We may feel guilty over our neglect of relatives or friends, especially when they need our help.

Our guilt may be caused by those situations where letters lie unanswered, tasks pile up undone, and journals lay on the desk with pages unturned for days or months or buried in a closet if one cannot bear the hammering reminder of not keeping up. This situation may cause some teachers, business women and men, doctors and nurses, computer programmers, lawyers, even pastors, to feel guilty about their inability to responsibly keep up with the knowledge explosion, the key issues, and new information for their productivity at work. This problem is a perpetual guilt hammering in many in the world today. It is commonly denied. It is frequently masked behind such comments as, "I'm sure glad I only have a couple of the years until retirement."

There are those times when we are often plagued and defeated by a sense of guilt over not being the kind of people we ought to be as God's daughters and sons in the global world. We have robbed others of happiness, meaningful relationship, patience, love, forgiveness, and a helping hand. We can feel hammering guilt and shame as consequences of these inner pangs of conscience. We can become weighed down in guilt. We can become unhappy. I have no doubt that our awareness of such guilt and shame, unrecognized and unrepented, is very destructive to our well-being. The feelings of guilt and shame drive us to be isolated from our real selves, others, and, most of all, God. Guilt and shame turn us against ourselves, away from others, and most likely away from Jesus, the Living Water that wells up to abundant living and to eternal life. Recognizing guilt and shame can be freeing. It contributes to healthier behavior patterns. They are good feelings for protecting and supporting our well-being and community. They may signal that a person or a racial group have not been recognized, affirmed, and supported as part of God's global family. Guilt makes us to hide from ourselves, others, and God, like Adam and Eve hid after their disobedient act in the garden of Eden. Guilt leads us toward self-reproach and self-rejection, which can lead to self-righteous judgment of others, if not abusing and rejecting them. Likewise, feelings of shame inhibit confession and our reconciliation with God and others.

If you have read portions of Shakespeare's writings, you are aware that he knew enough of the Bible and psychology to recognize that people can become sick from unconfessed guilt and associated feelings of shame. The memory of the murder of Duncan led to Lady Macbeth's "wasting away." When Macbeth asked the physician about his wife's illness, the physician replied, "Not so sick, my lord, as she is troubled with thick-coming fancies that keep her from rest." The same question can be put to many physicians today and was perhaps reflected in the dialogue between the woman at Jacob's well and Jesus, "Can you not minster to a mind diseased, pluck from the memory a rooted sorrow, raze out the troubles of the brain and with some sweet oblivious antidote cleanse the stuffed bosom of that perilous stuff which weighs upon the heart?"

It is a mistake to assume or to think that a recognition of guilt or a sense of shame is bad. I would rather encourage one to believe that recognizing these feelings is the beginning of change, repentance, healing, and hope toward more abundant living. These feelings recognized, utilized, and resolved appropriately can be beneficial and contribute to a healthy well-being. How then do we find forgiveness for our guilt-causing acts and our sense of shame? The account of the woman at Jacob's well speaks to this question of our need. We see here our daily need to be recognized, to be loved, and to be affirmed with worth and dignity regardless of our acts and condition. This account tells us that the relationship between God and all human beings is rooted in love and grace.

Our weekly liturgy in most worship settings addresses our need to be accepted, forgiven, and prized as the forgiven ones in our daily lives and in God's forever family:

> "If we confess our sins, he is faithful and just to forgive us our sins and to cleanse us from all unrighteousness." (1 John 1:9 ESV)

> "The Lord bless you and keep you; the Lord make his face shine upon you and be gracious to you; the Lord lift up his countenance upon you and give you peace." (Num. 6:24–26 ESV)

Faith holds on to God's daily unconditional love and grace. The grace for the woman at Jacob's well is seen as God's incredible acceptance of each human being through forgiving love. God's forgiveness speaks to and covers all our guilt acts, all our deserved feelings of shame, and the hammering judgment of others around us. God's grace to us says that neither self-accusations nor self-disgust can separate us from the love of God. The woman at Jacob's well heard and experienced that forgiving love. She was freed indeed. In hearing and experiencing Jesus's acceptance and affirming forgiveness, she left with excited joy, forgetting her water jar at the well. She hurried back to her city to tell the people what she had experienced at midday with Jesus at Jacob's well.

What Jesus came to say and demonstrate to the woman, to the world (John 3:16), and to us, Apostle Paul reminds us in his letter to the Romans (chapter 9) that even if our feelings of guilt and shame are against us, God is always for us. Nothing can separate us from the love of God toward us through Jesus of Nazareth's life, death, and resurrection. Guilt from our acts and the shame it can arouse shall have no final power over us or on our future. No self-scorn, no loss of dignity, no broken condition, or no imperfect scorecard shall separate us from the love of God as seen in, taught, and acted out by Jesus.

To be accepted as a person, to be loved despite of our acts, and to be in God's family now and forever, despite any guilt acts or weighty shame, is a burning thirst in every stage of life. So remember Jesus's conversation with the woman at Jacob's well.

"You are not only fully known, you are fully loved, and you are forgiven. Lift up your face. See yourself in the clear water that I have given you. Your redemption is near at hand! The Lord looks upon you with favor and gives you peace" (author's note).

## The Journey Verse

"Come to me, all you who are weary and burdened, and I will give you rest. Take my yoke upon you and learn from me, for I am gentle and humble in heart, and you will find rest for your souls."

(Matt. 11:28–29 NIV)

# Chapter 5

# Rest for Our Fatigue

*Come to me, all who labor and are heavy laden,
and I will give you rest. Take my yoke upon you, and
learn from me, for I am gentle and lowly in heart,
and you will find rest for your souls. For my yoke is
easy, and my burden is light.*
                        —Matthew 11:28–30 (ESV)

The fifth feeling we will discuss in this chapter is fatigue. Fatigue sounds too familiar, too undesirable, and too negative to be included in this book. Fatigue is one of a variety of feelings included in our birth package by God's design. Like all our feelings, fatigue is neither good nor bad. Our feelings are neutral until how they are affirmed, used, or expressed. How we get fatigued or how we respond to fatigue may be bad for us, our relationships, and our health and well-being. Like our other feelings, fatigue may manifest itself in negative and unhealthy ways. We should take time out from our tasks or work, listen to some relaxing music, do a meditation exercise, or take a slow walk on a favorite path. How many times have we heard this good advice from McDonald's, the favorite stopping place for a break under the Golden Arches, "You deserve a break today!"

Maybe that is why God put fatigue into the original design of our creation. We are told in the Creation story in Genesis 2:2–3 that God rested after he created the heavens and the earth. On the seventh day, God finished the work and rested from all the work he had done. God blessed the seventh day. God took a break after the six workdays. He set the example. The admonition to keep a rest day holy is for our good. It is a day to replenish physically, emotionally, and spiritually. It is a day to praise God for all we have and enjoy so abundantly along life's journey.

What fatigue-causing experiences do you remember? What causes fatigue in your daily journey? I knew fatigue from my paper route as a young boy from the heavy weight of newspapers. The pages were much larger and widely circulated, especially the Sunday edition of the *Des Moines Iowa Register* and *Des Moines Iowa Tribune*. I was the only paperboy for Slater, a small Iowa farm town. Carrying about eighty papers in a shoulder bag got me in touch daily with fatigue in my early boyhood days. I knew fatigue from playing my best in running after a long fly ball in center field. I knew what it was like to be fatigued after our using a full court press or running the fast breaks in basketball games. I always appreciated our coach taking a time-out to strategize the next plays in a close game. I knew fatigue from my long summer days of carpentry work, starting in seventh grade and through my high school years, to earn and save money for college. I have known the fatigue of helping care for a sick child throughout the night when rest was needed after a long day of work. I knew fatigue in the battle to recover from major surgery for melanoma cancer, intensified by the worry of whether or not I would survive and be able to return to work to help provide for my young family.

We each can build such a list from our lifetime of memories, from the past week, or from the past twenty-four hours. We can quickly identify with this feeling. Fatigue can be our daily friend, if we will listen to it. It becomes our enemy if we will not listen to it or if we deny the signals. Ignoring these warnings over long periods of time can lead to negative consequences in our physical, emotional, and spiritual well-being.

The stories in the Bible never make our common distinction between work and fatigue. That is true, whether the references are to weariness from a long day's work, a long journey, or a burdensome situation. In John 4:6, Jesus is seated beside Jacob's well, weary from a journey. In Luke 5:4–6, some fishermen told Jesus, "We wearied all night and took nothing." They were fatigued and needed rest. However, Jesus told the disappointed, frustrated fishermen, "Go out into deeper water! Cast your nets out on the other side of the boat." Unsurprisingly, fatigue comes from working hard and becoming tired. This feeling signals the need for refreshment, rest, and renewal of strength and energy. The same words for work and fatigue were used by people in Jesus's day. They labored under the laws of their religion, under rules and expectations in their rituals and worship life. Jesus's teaching about the Sabbath laws and rest in Matthew 12 strikes a responsive note in us.

Life is not easy. For the most part, living is hard. Keeping rules is even harder work. Trying to meet all expectations and to be perfect is a burden. It is a wearisome yoke under which we long for rest. However, life does carry with it marvelous possibilities for joys and satisfaction each day. There is great joy and satisfaction in the day's tasks done well, a special project or report completed on time, a new house constructed with quality work, a caring deed done with love and compassion, or an act of worship faithfully expressed or presided over. One finds purpose and meaning in life being productive. One finds satisfaction, even rest and refreshment, by giving our time and effort. This happens through many forms of work, play, and worship.

Daily work, however, is nothing but a series of laborious tasks and burdens. Most people throughout the world are bound so firmly to the economic wheel. The wheel spins faster and faster, demanding more and more in our American culture today. We work harder, faster, and longer days just to make ends meet. Many individuals, couples, and parents are compelled to work two jobs just to keep up, especially with children to support, ever-increasing cost of living, essential expenses, higher mortgages or rent (often for smaller houses and apartments), health care expenses, costly medicines, and mounting credit card debts. Most workers have no prospect of a lighter yoke or rest from being fatigued. Sabbath breaks and rest days become even more essential in maintaining health and well-being—physically, emotionally, and spiritually.

In Matthew 11:28–30, 12:1–14, Jesus invites rest from fatigue. What kind of fatigue does Jesus have in mind Remember that Jesus told those disciples to get back out on the lake to deeper water and fish longer for a big catch, "Get the task done!" Jesus was not calling people to a free lunch, as if he intended to continue feeding them daily by multiplying loaves of bread and borrowed fish. The rest that Jesus was talking about was not a rest from physical work or the relaxation that follows the refreshing fatigue from a fast handball game, swimming laps, a yoga exercise class, or a long evening walk alone, with your dog, or a special friend in the moonlight. We were created in the image of God to be creators, doers, and workers. The fatigue from recreation and fun activities is just a part of the process of being refreshed and renewed in healthy living.

The writers of the opening chapters of Genesis expressed this view in these words, "The Lord God took the man and put him in the garden of Eden to till it and keep it" (Gen. 2:15). God said to them, "Be fruitful and multiply, and fill the earth and subdue it; and have dominion over every living thing that moves upon the earth" (Gen. 1:28, paraphrase). To have dominion is the awesome responsibility and laborious work as being the caretaker of all living things on this earth. We are not very responsible in fulfilling that task at the beginning of the twenty-first century. We are overconsuming living things, polluting the oxygen we need to breathe, and destroying our global environment. We are not to live out our days only in consumption. We are to take care of our earth garden. This commission and work imply that we are to sustain and to keep our home alive. Jesus's calling in this gospel scene in no way changes this responsibility and its mammoth task.

Can we know for sure the nature of the burdens mentioned in this passage from which Jesus had the authority to free us? In his words, Jesus proposed the substitution of "his yoke" for the burdens being carried by those whom he summoned to follow him. After proposing "his yoke," Jesus added, "Learn from me." Jesus is presenting his own teaching to them as his disciples or yoke-bearers, that the wearisome burdens in question were not unrelated to a "teaching" or to a "way of living" under which the people to whom Jesus was talking were already living daily as wearisome and heavy burden. It was killing both their spirits and their bodies.

Jesus—the Way, the Truth, and the Life—is about showing us God's free gifts of forgiveness and life eternal, "Come to me, all you that are weary and are carrying heavy burdens, and I will give you rest... I am gentle and humble in heart, and you will find rest for your souls" (John 11:28). What this invitation for rest is rally telling us is. "Come unto me all of you who have been working so hard at saving yourselves. Know that I *am* your salvation." This understanding of Jesus's invitation is confirmed by the context in which it is placed. The next narrative immediately after this one refers to the hungry disciples picking up and eating grain as they passed through a field on the Sabbath. They were eating from someone else's grain field or vineyard. That was not a wrong act in their day and accepted as their custom. Well, the Pharisees observed what Jesus's disciples were doing and rebuked Jesus and his disciples for breaking one or two of the laws in "their teaching." Jesus said to the Pharisees, "The Son of Man is the Lord of the Sabbath" (Matt. 12:8). "The Sabbath was made for man, not man for the Sabbath" (Mark 12:27 NIV).

The Pharisees and the doctors of the law and the scribes in Jesus's day placed on each person's shoulders a burden. Each person's relationship with God depended on fulfilling about 613 commandments. These laws had to be scrupulously obeyed, especially those concerning the observance of the Sabbath. If any of the laws were disregarded or broken, they threaten condemnation and rejection from both religious and social activities in the community. The basic discipline principle was, "Whoever transgressed the smallest commandment transgressed them all!" This was the worrisome yoke that they could be set free from by Jesus. There could never be any peace of mind and promise of favor under any other teaching. One was never certain of fulfilling with perfection the 613 commandments in acts and in spirit. Jesus's words and invitation set them, and us, free from this burdensome way, "Learn from me! I will give you rest! My burden is light!"

Whoever transgressed the commandments became a sinner. That person would be cut off from the religious community. This is what happened to the publicans in Jesus's day. They were Jews who handled the money and taxes bearing the image of Caesar. This was also a forbidden act in their 613 rules and boundaries. The Pharisees attacked, judging Jesus and his disciples, applying their own double standards. Jesus's admonition is to judge not! Leave the judgment to God. A judgmental person only adds to the wearisome fatigue. In Jesus's invitation, we live out our daily journey in a new freedom where God's love and grace set us free. Thus, people who were already exhausted by their daily work were further oppressed by their religion. But Jesus announces a new way, a new day: Rest has come from that folly. "Learn from me! I am gentle and caring in heart! You will find rest!"

This feeling of fatigue is one of God's gifts to us in our birth package and even seen in the life of Jesus during his earth journey. Fatigue can turn us to rest and to refreshing activities to nourish our well-being. Fatigue can turn us to find peace in God. It can make us participate in a worship community around word and sacraments or turn us into a pathway of meditation. These set us free in the abiding presence, love, and grace of the inviting Jesus, "Come unto to me. I am with you always. I will give you rest!"

This peace that Jesus brings into our lives is not an earned reward. It is not a recognition at the end of life for our perfect work, sacrifice offerings, and worship along life's journey. Peace with God, freedom from our wearisome burdens of work, guilt, and shame, or from whatever cause is a blessing. It is granted upon us now through Jesus's life-blood and right-living for us. This peace is a condition in our inner being that is filled by God's presence, love, and grace. It is a light yoke! It is a light burden. It is life giving! Our names are written in the book of life by the blood shed by the Lamb on the cross. Our names are etched forever on the cross as citizens in God's future community.

One of Jesus's tasks was to convince people that *rest has come* when we recognize the impossibility of living a perfect life. We cannot earn or deserve, even in faithful living and worship, the gift of life eternal. It fact, both legalism and salvation by works are idolatries. It is a denial of the very one in whose image each one of us is modeled after. It is only when we recognize and affirm this truth about ourselves that we get to live in and under the easy yoke of Jesus. It is only then that we will want to learn from Jesus. It is only then that we are free to follow in the teachings and in the light of Jesus's way. It is only then that we will know that by faith, we are already forgiven and always will be forgiven. Indeed, we know that, even in our fatigue, our past is past, the burning is burnt. We are new creatures in Jesus. Our future is eternally open! We are in every moment, in every day, and in every stage of life's journey: Easter people in a Good Friday kind of world! Rest has come! Know this rest and live in it daily!

## The Journey Verses

Rejoice in the Lord always, again I will say, Rejoice. Let your gentleness be known to everyone. The Lord is near. Do not be anxious about anything, but in every situation, by prayer and petition with thanksgiving present let your requests be made known to God. And the peace of God, which transcends all understanding, will guard your hearts and your minds in Christ Jesus.
(Phil. 4:4–7 NIV)

I know what it is to be in need, and I know what it is to have plenty. I have learned the secret of being content in any and every situation, whether well fed or hungry, whether living in plenty or in want. I can do all this through him who gives me strength.
(Phil. 4: 12–13 NIV)

# Chapter 6

# *The Monster Within as Fear*

*Two men went up to the temple to pray, one a Pharisee and the other a tax collector. The Pharisee stood by himself and prayed: "God, I thank you that I am not like other people..." But the tax collector stood at a distance. He would not even look up to heaven, but beat his breast and said, "God, have mercy on me, a sinner!"*
—Luke 18:10–13 (NIV)

We continue our reflections on various natural feelings as we are designed in the image of our Creator. If fatigue sounded too negative and undesirable to be considered as one of our feelings in our birth package, then fear sounds equally undesirable. Like our other feelings, fear is natural and neutral. Fear is neither good nor bad until felt and acted upon. Rational fear is a part of our life. Baseless, projected, and exaggerated fears, regardless of their source of origin and content, can become like monsters within us that can hold us hostage. If unnamed, denied, and not dealt with, they can cause harm in our physical, emotional and spiritual well-being, greatly affecting and limiting our functional and abundant living in every arena of life's journey, especially in our relationships, work, play, and worship.

As a science major in college, I learned in my anatomy courses as a premedical student that the amygdala, a little control center in our brain, triggers and processes our fears. Once activated by whatever source and stimulus, the action may be for our good or for our harm. Fears can protect us. Fears can paralyze and depress us. Fears can hold us hostage. Fears unrecognized, unnamed, untreated, and unresolved can lead us down a pathway to despondency, depression, and, if prolonged, despair.

Fear is no stranger to any of us. What are your fears? What experiences do you remember when you were afraid? Falling into the deep end of the swimming pool or standing at the tip of the sixteen-foot diving board? Painting from the top of a high ladder? Taking a hot casserole out of the oven or reaching for a cake box stored on a high shelf? Asking out someone or being asked for a date over the phone? Seeing a speeding car in the rear-view mirror coming up too close to you or nearly missing a stoplight? Visiting the dentist or the oncologist? Giving a talk to a small group of strangers or experts in your profession or addressing a massive audience? Pause here. Take a break to open your memory box. What are some of your fear experiences?

Fear is our friend when it triggers actions to be cautious or careful; to be protective or defensive; and to seek assistance or care from doctors and nurses, psychologists and spiritual directors, and life coaches and pastors. Jesus teaches us insights in many of his parables to see, name, and tame our fear monsters. Jesus's parables give us healing for our fears so that we might live our journey days in abundance and face our future with confidence and peace. Jesus not only taught parables, his whole life was a parable for us. His life was a God-given parable about each of our own life stories, from our birth—through our journey days and experiences—to our last breath. Like Jesus's words in his last breath, we are to utter, "Father, into your hands I commend my spirit" (Luke 23:46). Then our story continues. Life after life! Jesus is risen indeed! In this sign, blessing, and promise, there is no rooming space for negative, harmful fear. We, too, are already the risen ones in Jesus's likeness. Like the promise we have in one of my favorite hymns, "Have No Fear, Little Flock," says:

*"Have no fear, little flock; have no fear, little flock,*
*for the Father has chosen to give you the kingdom;*
*have no fear, little flock! Have good cheer, little*

*flock; have good cheer, little flock, for the Father will keep you in his love forever; have good cheer, little flock"* (Evangelical Lutheran Worship Book, hymn 764, verses 1–2).

Feeling fear does not make us unworthy in God's family. We may think we are not good enough. We may think that we are not acceptable as we are, that we are likely among the rejected ones, like the tax collector in Jesus's parable. We will give special consideration in this chapter for the parable of the Pharisee and the tax collector at prayer in the temple. How we handle our self-image and feelings, especially our feelings concerning our relationships with others and with God, is an important concern in self-care and soul-care. The tax collector in Jesus's parable was beating his chest and beating himself down, likely in tears. How and why we get despondent and depressed is important to be recognized, resolved, and treated professionally before the monster becomes despair. How we ignore, deny, or delay facing fears that have become monsters, holding us hostage, can be harmful to our well-being and our relationship to ourselves, others, and God.

In my experience providing pastoral care and spiritual guidance, I have often heard others express in feelings, actions, and words, "I'm hurting inside! I'm feeling down. I just can't get in gear. I feel like I am lost in a dark tunnel. I feel so alone! I feel out of touch with God." These expressions are likely signals of fear. I remember an attractive young couple in my parish in Ohio. Both were professionals in their chosen careers. They were buying a beautiful new house, and each had a brightly colored sport car. The couple finally had a baby girl after seven years of trying to start a family. This represented the fulfillment of some of their deepest needs and hopes. At first, the couple was radiantly happy with the new arrival. About six months later, the wife became deeply depressed. She had many severe headaches, cried often, lost weight, and neglected herself and her family. The emotional demands placed on her by her own expectations about what she should be able to do as a good mother and continue her professional career were becoming exhausting. Adding to this burden was her projected perception and experiences of the expectations of others around her. She was becoming paralyzed in her fear. She was afraid that she was failing, that she was not capable of being a good mother and a successful career woman. Her husband soon followed in this downward spiral and entered the dark night of depression. The wife started blaming herself for causing her husband's depression. Her fear of losing her husband became an added monster in her life.

Real, projected, and exaggerated fears affect people of all ages. It occurs in all social groups in congested urban areas and in the open countryside. It occurs in both sexes often. Unfortunately, many people suffer in silence what I call the three Ds—despondency, depression, and despair. They often blame themselves for not being perfect in who they are and what they are able do, whatever their roles, relationships, and work might be. They blame themselves for not being able to pick themselves up out of their wells of darkness. They forget or do not understand that this is impossible, especially when negative and destructive fear monsters hold us hostage.

Furthermore, Jesus's cross of deliverance would not have been necessary if it were within our capabilities and possible for any one of us to act perfectly in all our roles, relationships, work, and activities in each stage of our life's journey. With the transforming and renewing work of the Spirit of God within us and the supportive care and guidance of doctors, psychologist, and counselors for the medical resources and therapy treatments they provide, we can resolve and conquer our binding fears to become freed, healed, and renewed for abundant living. What then is the function of fear? This feeling points us to our deeper needs. It points us to the love, acceptance, support, and freedom we see in Jesus's way that we must affirm and practice daily toward ourselves, our family, our friends, and the community around us where we live, work, and worship.

Having said this, we also must acknowledge that life is difficult. Monster fears can be brought on by the trauma of loss, sickness, and diseases, especially the likes of the COVID-19 pandemic. Fears, real or projected, that can become harmful monsters in our daily living include, among others, the loss of identity, self-confidence, dignity, a significant person or relationship, work position or role in the community, and a relationship with God. Fear can be brought on by the loss of faith, an absence, or rejection of God. Many of our fears seem to occur for no obvious or explainable reason. From a medical viewpoint, doctors may say that despondency and depression are a manifestation of a neurochemical imbalance in the brain. Some doctors would also say that the tendency is hardwired into one's genetic makeup. Therefore, the tendency for being present and expressed is inherited. Fears manifested from this origin are viewed as an illness to be managed by drugs, diet, and stress management techniques.

Fear expressed in the three Ds is prominent among the declared feelings in biblical personalities. The Psalms reflect the highs and lows of human existence. The mood in one psalm might be, "Make a joyful noise to the Lord" (Psalm 98). In the next psalm, "I am weary of my crying; my throat is parched…while I wait for my God" (Psalm 69:3). Many Bible stories echo the expressed feeling of fears in despondency and despair. The description of such feelings is told without placing upon them a negative value. They are shared as normal expressions in some circumstances.

Ask these persons what seasons and circumstances their prosperity of joy, blessing, and deliverance came from:

- *Ask Abraham.* He will point you to offering up of his son Isaac as a burnt offering.
- *Ask Moses.* He will point you back to his dark fears, wandering through the wilderness until his death, "Kill me at once…that I may not see my wretchedness."
- *Ask Job.* He would describe himself as one who is "bitter in soul," cursed the day of his birth from his mother's womb, and longed for death until he was delivered from his despair, saying, "I know that my Redeemer lives!"
- *Ask Ruth.* She will bid you to build her monument in the field of her toil and long season of despair.
- *Ask David.* He will tell you that many of his songs came from his nights of fear, his disappointments, depression, and despair.

We see those same dark moments in the life of Jesus. Jesus wept over Jerusalem. He wept at the death of his close friend, Lazarus. He struggled in the dark shadows of Gethsemane in disillusionment and despair, hoping for a different solution for his impending death on the cross when Jesus cried, "My God, my God, why have you forsaken me?" (Matt. 27:46).

Faced with fears in these biblical stories we know all too well today, we might ask ourselves: Does fear have some necessary, helpful role to play in life's journey? Why do we have such a feeling in our birth package by God's design? How can fears with any source of manifestation work for good? How might fears be an ally by God's purpose in the design?

Some feelings and thoughts in our daily experiences may manifest in a dark mood. Deny or suppress the mood; suppress the thoughts, words, or deeds, and you will soon be held hostage by them. They will be harmful to one's well-being (physically, emotionally, and spiritually) and to one's relationships and productivity as well as happiness and abundant living. This suppression can lead to separation from one's real self, from God, from significant relationships, and from the community. This separation can be destructive to both life and faith. Expressed fear, however, may be positive. They may be an important channel for managing and resolving "negative feelings," just as expressed affection is for the emotion of love. Expressed love can manifest as gestures, acts of concern, care, and attachment. If denied and not expressed, the potential darkness of some fears can evoke an awareness and an articulation of thoughts that would remain hidden behind the screen of our lighter moods and denials. They hold our inner self hostage and become destructive. Expressed fears can lead to a renewed peace, healing, and strength. It can lead to a blessing of acceptance and forgiveness from being loved rather than being perfect based on a gift assurance as given to us by Jesus.

The unnamed publican in Jesus's parable in Luke 18:9–14 knew this feeling of fear. He had come to the end of himself, beating himself down. If the publican had been like so many others in his day and ours, he could have blamed his condition and his state of fears on his family background, his genetic predisposition, his educational upbringing in his community, his environment or circumstances of needing a job, or even on his sinful companions. He feared rejection. He feared not being worthy and not being acceptable to God. Respectable people in Jesus's day, like the critical Pharisee standing off to the side, despised publicans. Would Jesus also despise him?

In the parable, taught by Jesus as a real-life illustration, the publican despised himself. Not only did he not blame his unfortunate fate on his depressed state of mind, he also laid no claim to any merit in God's sight. His prayers, his fasting, and his tithing, according to his strict observance of the Law, was not working anymore for his weekly deliverance and peace of mind. The publican knew himself and his need. He knew that he was an unjust tax collector, an "extortioner," and a sinner. The publican could only blame himself and pray, "God, be merciful to me, a sinner" (Luke 18:13). God had mercy on the publican instantly! In the parable, the publican went down to his house forgiven and justified. In the publican's discouragement, in his struggle against himself, in his fear feeling of not being worthy or acceptable, he was despairing and depressed that if there be no mercy from God, he was irretrievably lost. This is the ultimate fear of being forever lost to life. In like fashion, those who are equally despondent, depressed, and despairing, they fear that they are utterly lost.

Like this repentant publican, being humble and seeing himself lost, not blaming others or claiming merit, one can also affirm in faith:

> "Out of the depths I have cried to You, O Lord. Lord, hear my voice! Let your ears be attentive to the voice of my supplications. If You, Lord, should mark iniquities, O Lord, who could stand? But there is forgiveness with You, that You may be feared" (Psalm 130:1–4 NASB).

Out of the dark fears, whether a night's struggle or a season's struggle against oneself, deliverance can come. As the psalmist would say, it is your mountains and hills that will break forth into singing. The trees of your silent forest will clap their hands (Isa. 55:12).

In our journey, there will likely be moments, days, and seasons of distress, discouragement, darkness, and despair. We must handle our pain and our fears through openness, confession, and support, even if we cannot fully identify and understand them. We must drain the inner swamp or we bury them alive. Because of the possibility of painful emptiness, like the publican beating his chest in the temple, we need to look for positive and helpful ways to face and resolve our fears. Maybe we need to broaden our vision here. Maybe we have to see that fear, the loss of familiar structures in life, the lack of enthusiasm, and the motivation to press forward are all signals that can turn us to the mercy, forgiveness, blessing of peace, and power to live abundantly as the Spirit of God works that healing and newness in us.

Helpless and hopeless is the person who, in that deep dark season, knows not who to turn to for professional care, treatment, and support, like the publican, cried out to God in Jesus's parable, "Lord, be merciful to me! Be helpful to me in my need!" Happy is the person, however dark the night, who has faith that God will not forsake him or her.

The scriptures teach us that some of our shortest prayers are our most honest and effective ones, like Jesus's short prayer in Gethsemane, "Lord, let this cup pass for me," and his seven short prayers on the cross. Remember and use Peter's short prayer every day in times of deep need or despair, "Lord, save me!" (Matt. 14:30).

Faith without feelings is dead to our awareness as a gift always within us from the Spirit's abiding presence. That is a promise! Jesus said, "Remember, I am with you always, to the end of the age" (Matt. 28:20). We are never abandoned. We may deny or abandon Jesus for years, but the Spirit of Jesus has a grip on us always, daily, and forever. He will present every last one of us before the throne of grace with exceedingly great joy. It is a fallacy to make certain feelings that we have be a test of faith, including the presence or absence of fear by our lack of recognition and affirmation.

Faith brings deliverance, healing, blessings, and hope. Faith can also bring emotional peace. This faith is not magical. Faith is real. Faith is the first gift of the Spirit of God, the Spirit of the risen Jesus, working within us and promising to make us and all things new. Faith does not override the feelings, including fear. Faith brings peace and rest! Faith is the strength to believe more than we feel and hope above the challenges, the desperations, and the impossibilities of life. Faith upholds us and empowers us to live through and survive the dark moments, days, and seasons, affirming with Job, "I know that my Redeemer lives" (Job 19:25). Faith is the strength to believe. With faith, our cries to the Lord about our fears bring us to the crown of deliverance, to healing, to victory, and to life anew in the likeness of the risen Jesus. Disciplined in faith by our fears, we come to know and trust the Deliverer through our life's journey, through the end times, and our resurrection at the throne of grace with exceedingly great joy!

# The Journey Verse

By this we know that we abide in Him and He in us, because He has given us of His Spirit. We have seen and do testify that the Father has sent the Son to be the Savior of the world. Whoever confesses that Jesus is the Son of God, God abides in him, and he in God... God is love, and the one who abides in love abides in God, and God abides in them... There is no fear in love; but perfect love casts out fear, because fear involves punishment, and the one who fears is not perfected in love. We love, because He first loved us.
(1 John 4:13–16, 18–19 NASB)

# Chapter 7

# *In Life's Whys, Where Is the Joy?*

*Now a certain man was ill, Lazarus of Bethany,
the village of Mary and her sister Martha. Mary
was the one who anointed the Lord with perfume
and wiped his feet with hair, whose brother Lazarus
was ill. So the sisters sent to him, saying, "Lord, he
whom you love is ill." But when Jesus heard it, he
said, "This illness does not lead to death. It is for the
glory of God, so that the Son of God may be glorified
through it... Then after this he said to the disciples,
"Let us go to Judea again." The disciples said to him,
"Rabbi, the Jews were just now seeking to stone you,
and are you going there again?" Jesus answered, "Are
there not twelve hours in the day? If anyone walks in
the day, he does not stumble, because he sees the light
of this world. But if anyone walks in the night, he
stumbles, because the light is not in them."*

—John 11:1–4, 7–10 (ESV)

In the previous chapters, we have explored such feelings as anxiety, doubt, anger, guilt, fatigue, and fear. We have acknowledged that these feelings are all a part of our birth package by God's design. They are reflective of God's essence within each one of us. In the opening chapter of Genesis 1:31, God declared our natural design as "very good." They can all be potentially used for good. In this chapter, we shall focus on joy, giving special attention to where the joy is in the midst of all the whys along life's journey.

I enjoyed working with children and youth in my parish ministry work, especially in the children's story time in the Sunday worship service, at summer Bible camp, and the many Habitat projects building houses in the Yakima Valley in Washington. Their questions, energy, foolishness, and banter would fill me with joy, sometimes bursting into laughter with them. The campers told me many jokes. I recall one such experience at Bible camp that pushed me to hilarious laughter. At mealtimes, I would encourage the campers to write a postcard note home to their family. As I came into the dining hall for one of the meals, a young boy came up to me and said, "Hey, Pastor Lou! Is writing on an empty stomach harmful?" Before I got out an answer, he very wittingly added with a big smile, "No, but on paper is better!"

Along with the Spirit's gifts (faith, love, and hope), joy is one of the distinguishable from being created in the image of God. The affirmation of this gift and its daily expressions from us in our dispositions, in the central spirit of our work, words, and actions, and as the undergirding strength in our challenges and sufferings, is sorely needed in our kind of world today. When I think of someone who beautifully manifests this joyful disposition, I think of our daughter, Katie Joy. Katie has reflected this joy from day one with her naturally glowing smile. It has continued through her years with her facial expressions, her words and laughter, her caring spirit, and her life's work through her counseling practice. However, we frequently find ourselves and others asking why too many people are guilty of dullness, coldness, and despondent spirit.

What nourishes your joy? What brings joy to your face, in your tone of voice and chosen words, or in your actions of sharing and giving to others? What triggers you to burst out laughing? Pause here to recall some of those experiences and situations. Is it that first smile and good morning greeting from your spouse or a significant friend? Is it that first cup of morning brew and breakfast served to you in bed? Is it your dog, like Lexi who dances for joy in circles and runs to play hide-in-seek before going outside for her potty break and walk? Is it that courteous driver who slows down a bit to let you enter the flowing traffic on the freeway as everyone is speeding to work? Is it those conversation times with a special family member, like Linda who always has a twinkle in her eyes and a slight smile, sharing her witty insights and friendly jabs? Is it that anticipated dinner out after a long, hard day of work? Is it that ballgame or that live musical on stage planned as an evening date? What keeps you in touch with your joy?

It is not always easy or comfortable to run the race of life through some hurdles and sufferings with joy and perseverance. This is especially so when the joy modeled for us by Jesus is associated with the cross. We are reminded that it was because of the brutal suffering Jesus endured from his arrest at the garden of Gethsemane to finding joy to face his arrest, trial, and death on the cross. Such impressions are created, at least in part, when we do not affirm or reflect this gift of joy. Not so with Jesus! The writer of the book of Hebrews in the New Testament declares, "Let us run with endurance the race that is set before us, looking to Jesus, the founder and perfecter of our faith, who for the joy that was set before him endured the cross" (Heb. 12:1–2 ESV)

One of the first commonly spoken words by children is, "Why? Why? Why?" Our children, from the earliest stages onward, are in good company with Mary and Martha, the disciples of Jesus, and Jesus himself. Remember Jesus's struggle at praying all night in Gethsemane while his disciples kept falling asleep despite being aware of the impending suffering their friend and teacher was about to face. Jesus was asking that very real human question, "Why, God? My God, why this way of the cross?" Then we have those heartbreaking words, "My God, my God, why have you forsaken me?" We find that probing, burning, wondering question of *why* in Job's three friends as they grilled Job, perhaps expecting his admissions of guilt after all he suffered, the loss of property, wealth, family, and even his health.

As we read through the scriptures, we are in good company for our struggle with the whys in life's journey. Toddlers struggle with more than a few bumps and bruises as they learn to walk and run safely. The terrible twos learn some limits and accept some nurturing guidance to avoid suffering from their boundless energy. Teenagers struggle with even deeper questions about self-identity and feelings. They struggle with values, attitudes, norms, and expectations they learn from their parents, church, peers, teachers, and coaches. Adults keep asking questions to get understanding, to cope, to get resolutions, and to survive.

I believe God invites our questions, our protests, our confessions, and our laments! "Nothing is new under the sun" is a common saying. Most questions are not new. We see stories in the Bible about struggles and laments about life experiences and situations. Sufferings, whatever they are in particular, leave us asking, "Where were you, God? Where were you when we needed you the most? Why did you allow this to happen? Where is your protective love?" These were the questions Mary and Martha asked Jesus when their brother Lazarus became seriously ill and died. Recall the scene when Jesus finally arrived at Mary and Martha's house. Mary ran out of the house, knelt before Jesus, and asked, "Lord, where were you? Why the delay in responding to our message? Lord, if you had been here, my brother would not have died" (John 11:32). We hear these same questions, these same pleas from human hearts centuries ago:

- From Job in the midst of his losses and suffering, "Why did I not perish at birth, and die as I came from the womb?" (Job 3:11).
- From the psalm writers in despair, "Why, O Lord, do you stand far off? Why do you hide yourself in times of trouble?" (Psalm 10:1).
- From King David when his life was threatened. We have the prayer-cry that Jesus uttered in agony, bearing the accumulative weight of all human sufferings, "My God, my God, why have you forsaken me? Why are you so far from saving me, from the words of my groaning?" (Psalm 22:1 ESV).

Yes, we need to ask our questions, however, we must also learn that there are *mysteries* in life, experiences and circumstances that cannot be rationalized away or logically explained. We need to acknowledge that there are limits to human understanding. Each individual example of suffering certainly cannot be traced to a specific wrong act or mistake or to the absence of God's presence, power, and caring love. We cannot rationalize away or change our suffering by blaming God. It does not follow that when we suffer, God is absent. Looking back at an experience or season of great suffering, have you felt God's enlightenment and growth? Put on your memory cap now and recall these experiences? Did God give you strength to cope, endure, or overcome a terrible situation? Did God slowly or quickly work a miracle for you that you most needed or give you an even better resolution, healing, or miracle?

There can be a renewed feeling of joy, comfort, and peace for each of us as we recall that the ministry of Jesus was marked by compassionate commitment to people who were suffering. Suffering people were attracted to Jesus. Those who were unable to walk were often carried to Jesus to be healed. The Pharisees accused him of doing such caring work on the Sabbath. From stories during Jesus's life, we see God not exercising his power over people as if they were like puppets on strings, yanking up all the good people before suffering could hit them. God abides with us through our sufferings. Jesus's ministry had a power stronger than the forces of evil and death itself. It is unleashed for good, for healing, and, eventually, for life anew.

As we grapple with suffering, and its impact on our gift of joy, it is ultimately on the cross that we can see most clearly the heart of God. An important factor in the good news for life's journey in this kind of world, as in Jesus's world and brutal death on the cross, is that God's presence is constantly in us, with us, and for us. We see in Jesus God's way of dealing with these realities is to keeping his promise, "Lo, I am with you always!" (Matt. 28:20). It is on the cross that Jesus, the Word that became flesh (John 1:1–5), most fully identifies with us by suffering for us. Jesus fully experienced being human, created in God's image, endured pain, horror, and suffering on the cross. Jesus was sorrowful! That meant God was sorrowful! Jesus died with loud cries and tears. That means God was also weeping for Jerusalem not seeing the Way in his Son. Jesus also swept outside of Lazarus's house before calling him back to life. As Jesus cried out, "My God, my God, why have you forsaken me?" (Mark 15:34). So did God weep for us, the God who created all things in the beginning with the Word (John 1:1–5).

It is here that we see clearly where the joy is in the whys of our life. It is when we see and remember the purpose and meaning of Jesus's suffering. It was for all of us, without exception! Apostle Paul's advice to the Colossians is a good advice for us today, "See to it that no one takes you captive through philosophy and empty deceit, according to human tradition, according to the elemental spirits of the world, and not according to Christ. For in him the whole fullness of deity dwells bodily, and you have come to fullness in him, who is the head of every ruler and authority...and when you were dead in trespasses...God made you alive together with him, having forgiven us all our trespasses, canceling the record of debt that stood against us with its legal demands" (Col. 2–8-10, 13–14). The joy is always in God's presence with us, as with Jesus suffering on the cross, feeling the spikes in his hands and feet, the piercing crown of thorns, the jabbing of the guard's spear into his side, the thirsting for a sip of water.

We must ask another question here, "Is the critical element in the suffering we experience the pain?" This is the essential question since we know that all suffering and pain cannot be eradicated by technology. Some new challenge and suffering always appears, sooner than later. It might even be a greater one than the global coronavirus pandemic. We hope for an announcement soon from one of the science research labs that is working day and night to fast-track an effective vaccine. When it comes, we will dance with joy on the streets around the globe. The reality is, however, that the pharmaceutical industries and our politicians in national and local positions cannot resolve all circumstances of suffering we shall encounter along life's journey. As helpful as they are in bringing comfort, support, and healing, often as if a miracle, our doctors and nurses as well as pastors and counselors in health centers cannot resolve all our sufferings—physically, emotionally, or spiritually.

In all fairness, I believe it must be admitted that pain itself—by which we feel and measure our physical, mental, and emotional suffering—does not constitute our greatest crisis. An example may be of help here. A little boy who is spanked by his father, even if done lightly, will cry out as if in great pain. Like Jesus crying out on the cross, "Daddy! Daddy! Why?" The pain is not so much physical as it is in the boy's feeling of a broken relationship with his father. It is the emotional suffering rather than the spanking. The same boy and father can be wrestling on the living room floor. The boy will endure much more pain than is in most physical spankings because he knows it is all in fun. It is with a different purpose and meaning in the wrestling that the boy faces the challenge in joy and laughter.

I am sure you can think of other examples. People continue to choose hard manual labor or high-risk jobs for the joy and satisfaction they feel in it. Men and women continue to volunteer to go to war and risk torture for the joy and honor they feel in it. Women and men continue to enter competitive sports, often with demanding training sessions, long days, and distance away from family and friends. They suffer even physical and emotional sufferings in playing the sport all for the joy and pride they feel in it. Given the proper psychological or spiritual motivation, pain frequently does not precipitate serious crises. As for Jesus, the joy set before him in the purpose and meaning of the cross enabled Jesus to endure its shame, pain, and suffering.

Technology has done much to lessen suffering in our daily lives, both at home and in our work-a-day world, in our automobiles, and in our hospitals and therapy clinics. We should be thankful, but what of the suffering that remains when technologies have reached their limits or a vaccine for life-threatening COVID-19 has not been discovered and rapidly produced for massive distribution? What then? The important question we need to face is where in all the technological wisdom, cures, or temporary relief is there an answer to the suffering inherent in the inner cry: "Why did this happen to me... to us?"

Only the person who can ask this question about suffering's ultimate meaning, not simply about its technological causes and cures, feels his or her real pain in any critical and freeing sense. She or he alone is the person who is open to a possible answer that enables one to see joy in the midst of the whys in her or his physical and emotional sufferings. Many who attempt to answer this question do so by involving God. However, too often they do so only to blame God. Ether God is good but weak, or God is strong but unfair.

To illustrate this point, a young mother of an eight-year-old boy lost her husband to a cruel disease. In tears, she cried out, "For eight years, I have taught my little boy that God is love! What shall I tell him now?" I feel pity that his mother thought now was the time to relinquish the very affirmation that was designated for just such a time. God is with us in our loss! God is love! Daddy has gone ahead of us into God's home.

How else could one ever explain the joy in Job's suffering? In the midst of his grief, despair, loss of family, and being all alone, the only joy that Job could hold on to was in his faith and trust that his Redeemer still lived. Job believed that his Redeemer would be with him in death and subsequent life beyond all losses and suffering. This is comforting to us as we recall this joy in Job as his strength and peace in his life's journey. Job's three closest friends failed to see, affirm, and share this same gift in themselves that could have supported Job.

There is comfort here for each of us as we recall scenes from the teaching and healing ministry of Jesus. It was marked by compassionate love and joy as he responded to the needs of people who were suffering in body, in mind, in emotions, and in lack of faith. They were from all walks of life. Jesus's ministry is stronger than the forces in our sufferings, including death itself. It is the power of joy! As we grapple with God and human suffering, we can see clearly the ways God is supporting, helping, and healing us in our why moments. We see then in Jesus that God's way in dealing with these realities is to be engaged with us in them. God does this by being the promise-keeper with us as with Jesus: "Lo, I am with you always!" One of Jesus's names is Emmanuel, meaning, "God is with us."

The New Testament as a witness to this truth for our why's would have to be distorted to support any position and teaching that suffering and pain are sent by God, that our suffering is good character building. Such position only adds to both mental and emotional sufferings that are inevitably and commonly found in God-rejecting, God-denying people. There is certainly little in most suffering that seems good and much in most suffering that we could all get along without. The answer for its presence is not in blaming or rejecting God. As the scriptures show us within Creation and in this life of suffering, there are destructive forces at work within us and around us in this world hat is yet to be healed, transformed, made new, and forever whole.

We have this promise that God will make all things new and whole as we have already been made new and whole in the risen Jesus. We have all this and much more to rejoice in and to live joyfully in our disposition, in our perspective on life, and in our words and actions. We can do this if we can identify what makes it so. This joy in life and joy in living, and the joy within us is the answer in the why questions. It is not the same as happiness, although we frequently interchange the words. Happiness is partly self-made: a happy home, a happy friendship, and happy at work. Happiness is the fruit of our efforts and our achievements, often done with others. However, we are not responsible for our joy! We are both recipients of this natural gift in our birth package and we are to be instruments of joy as Jesus was the pioneer and perfecter of our faith and model for abundant living. As the Spirit of Living God, the risen Jesus, we are called and empowered to love, to work, to serve, to live joyfully, and to laugh with gladness of spirit.

We are to do this so that our joy may be full, in just being aware of life; in the moments of joy in love experienced in the flesh as well as in the spirit; in the moments of joy in the unbelievable beauty of the world; in the moments of joy in being found by someone when lonely, lost, or at life's end; in the moments of joy in realizing and feeling how great God's love and grace are; in the moments of joy that are ours when we come to realize that all things are in God's hands, including us, and in the moments of joy that well up when we really reach the dawn of what it means that God summons us to the new dance of life with Jesus, a life without end.

Joy is always a gift of God. It is our power source in the whys along our journey. This is a true presence whether we recognize it and express it or not. Joy is a gift of God—whether through his Creation, through his Son, through the bread and wine of the Supper, blessed, broken and given for us, or through sharing in another person's life. But joy is always a gift of God's presence! As is love! God is love! Those who abide in love, abide in God, and God abides them! We are the recipients and the instruments of joy, but all joy is ultimately God's. Even as all light on this earth ultimately derives from the light of the sun, all joy is from God. Even as that joy was in the God-embodied flesh and blood of Jesus, it enabled Jesus to endure the cross, for our salvation and our daily empowerment that we might not grow weary or faint-hearted in and through our whys along the race of our journey.

Behold the gift in you! Affirm the gift in you! Be the gift lived daily, joyfully!

## The Journey Verse

And let us run with endurance the race that is set before us, fixing our eyes on Jesus, the author and perfecter of our faith, who for the joy set before him endured the cross, despising the shame, and has sat down at the right hand of the throne of God. For consider him who has endured such hostility by sinners against Himself, so that you will not grow weary and lose heart.

(Heb. 12:1–3 NIV)

# Chapter 8

# *Back to the Future Now in Peace*

*Now there was a Pharisee named Nicodemus who was a member of the Jewish ruling council. He came to Jesus at night and said, "Rabbi, we know that you are a teacher who has come from God. For no one can perform the signs you are doing if God were not with him." Jesus replied, "Very truly I tell you, no one can see the kingdom of God unless they are born again."... "Very truly I tell you, no one can enter the kingdom of God unless they are born of water and the Spirit."... "No one has ever gone into heaven except the one who came from heaven—the Son of Man. Just as Moses lifted up the serpent in the wilderness, so the Son of Man must be lifted up, that everyone who believes may have eternal life in him." For God so loved the world that he gave his one and only Son, that whoever believes in him shall not perish but have eternal life. For God did not send his Son into the world to condemn the world, but to save the world through him.*
—John 3:1–3, 5, 13–17 (NIV)

In our birth package of natural feelings by the Creator's design, we were given one special feeling that is our deepest emotional need along our life's journey, peace. Peace is our strongest feeling. If not felt, experienced, and expressed, there is a deep sense of disconnection from self, from others, and even from God. If peace is disrupted or not supported, for whatever reason, there is a deep longing for peace, even against hope. Perhaps that is why infants cry at birth, not primarily because of pain in the birthing process but because they sense their first separation. If one's peace is not felt and expressed in one's daily life; one's vision of the world; one's joys and hopes; one's longings for satisfaction in relationships, work, and activities; and one's needs for abundant living, all can be found wanting in the balance of well-being.

From early childhood, we hope that we are loved, wanted, and accepted. If not, we are not at peace. We hope to pass from first grade into second grade. If we do not pass, there are likely tears. We are not happy about the news. We will have lost—at least for some moments, if not for days—our sense of peace. This experience with peace continues with our hope of passing junior high into high school, from high school into college, and then successfully into some career path. We continue to hope for experiences and successes that affirm and support our peace. We know that feeling as *being at peace with one's self!* A yes to a movie or dinner invitation, a proposed project by your manager at work, or a marriage proposal. A yes to suggested plans for a new house, a cruise or vacation in Hawaii, or starting a family or adopting an infant. What would be on your "being at peace" list, for starters?

There is peace in all these kinds of life experiences. We hope for peace within ourselves, our families, friendships, communities, country, and other nations sharing this one big living room we call planet Earth. Violence in any form—from emotional and physical abuse, from shootings on the streets and in our schools to riots and warfare between any groups of people and nations—disrupts and destroys peace. Violence is an enemy of peace. It takes affirming our peace within and a longing for peace lived, expressed, and shared to endure in the wanting, waiting times, and battles and to survive until peace is shared, supported, and celebrated by all in our homes, communities, country, and nations. Peace involves our whole being.

Lack of peace affects our well-being, physically, emotionally, and spiritually.

We have all read stories about ships and people lost at sea. I remember being caught by a sudden summer storm in my small fishing boat in the middle of a lake in Northern Minnesota. The wind whipped up slamming waves that almost turned the boat over several times before I reached shore safely. Fear quickly overshadowed the calm peace I felt that day, fishing on the lake. Such stories and personal experiences remind me of the vivid account of the Apostle Paul's shipwreck in Acts chapter 27. Paul was on his way to Rome when a massive storm rolled in. The account reads:

> *Since we were violently storm-tossed, they began the next day to jettison the cargo. And on the third day they threw the ship's tackle overboard with their own hands. When neither sun nor stars appeared for many days, and no small tempest lay on us, all hope of our being saved was at last abandoned.* (Acts 27:18–20 ESV)

Lack of hope is the overshadowing of our peace. To Apostle Paul and his crew, it seemed their chance of survival was slim. The shipwreck crew was at the mercy of the storm. Peace was exactly what the crew wanted while their small wooden vessel was violently tossed in the storm. They wanted to anchor themselves to ride out the storm, however high the waves might have tossed them. We all want an anchor to withstand our storms in life.

What are some of your experiences that threaten or disrupt your peace? Is it your neighbor's dog loudly barking? Is it a child running late for the bus stop? Is it the news of another school shooting scaring you to send your child off to school? Is it the rising number of gun sales with little or inadequate background checks? Is it the daily news of mistreatment of migrants at our southern borders, separating parents from children and keeping them in crowded cages without soap and adequate clean clothes? Is it your oncologist telling you the frightening news that you have stage 4 cancer? Is it the stay-at-home order because of COVID-19 along with your unemployment notice and the phone call that says a coworker or friend contracted coronavirus? What are your peace disrupters? What is your anchor in these daily storm realities, whether they be little or big? Now I ask the questions again, why is peace like an anchor? What is the basis of our peace that enables us to stand strong during the disappointments, disruptions, and tragedies along life's journey?

Before I tell you my answer to these questions, I must first state that the peace referred in the Bible is anchored in God's person and nature, seen by those who have "eyes to see and ears to hear." It is rooted in their faith-stories through the centuries. It is rooted in their belief that God created all things and that we are created in the image of God. Jesus, the "Word that became flesh," was born from Mary's womb and grew up in Joseph and Mary's house in Nazareth. For starters, peace is not primarily an outward condition created, disrupted, or taken away by humans. It is not just an emotional feeling or a hopeful wish. It is not a calculated security. Peace is a natural feeling in our birth package of feelings designed by God, reflecting God's personal image and essence. As a natural feeling, peace exists within us not only from how we feel or on how we see its expressions. Peace is a part of our natural being and essence. Like Jesus, each one of us is created in God's image. Jesus not only taught parables. His whole life was a parable for our own stories. We see in Jesus's story as a parable for each of our own stories, as daughters and sons of the Creator, the meaning, value, purpose, and direction of our lives from birth, through life's journey and through death, to life anew in Jesus's likeness. We see here the origin, basis, and anchor of our peace in whose we are. It is seen in the image given to us in our birth package.

Peace does not appear and disappear depending on our emotions. It is established on a future joy experienced now. It is seen then in Jesus's story as the parable of each of our own stories, from its beginning, its experiences and feelings along the way, to its apparent ending in God's eternal future. We are told of certain peace by Peter:

*Blessed be the God and Father of our Lord Jesus Christ! By his great mercy he gave us new birth into a living hope through the resurrection of Jesus Christ from the dead, that is, into an inheritance imperishable, undefiled, and unfading. It is reserved in heaven for you, who by God's power are protected through faith for a salvation ready to be revealed in the last time.* (1 Pet. 1:3–5 NET)

Back to the future joy is our basis and anchor for peace in all situations and seasons of life's journey. From Jesus's death and resurrection, clearly God's anchor for us is Jesus who promised, "Lo, I am with you always, to the end of the age" (Matt. 28:20). Our future joy is seen in these past events. Those events turn our peace from being just a hope fulfilled or a calculated resolution being successful by our self-efforts or the efforts of others for which we get the credit and some relief satisfaction. Peace is our natural power. Peace is our anchor. Peace enables us to face all the situations in life and embrace each day with joy. It gives us the basis of our strength, our endurance, and our hope in all seasons and situations and in the dark passage of death. We often hear people say, "Grandma passed away so peacefully!" or "He is at peace now!" about someone who fought the good fight against a longsuffering illness.

What is that living peace that is our sure birthright? It is the sure peace that life as we know it and experience it is experienced, supported, enabled, and blessed by the risen Jesus, the Spirit, tenting within us and making our journey with us. Whatever the happenings are, nearby or far away, locally or globally, our lives, though disrupted often and perhaps appearing hopeless or defeated at times, will not end in defeat and nothingness. The journey ends in life anew in salvation. That gift and promise sign was prepared for us by God in Jesus's teachings, "For God so loved the world that he gave his only Son, so that everyone may have eternal life... God did not send the Son into the world to condemn the world, but in order that the world might be saved through him" (John 3:16–17). That gift, an anchor for our peace, will be revealed in our last passage when we are welcomed home into God's eternal future.

This security is revealed in the nature and promises embodied and lived out by Jesus. It was already reflected in that pre-Christian hope that runs throughout the Old Testament. Probably the most significant act of God in that first covenant period is called to remembrance by Jesus with Nicodemus when he questioned Jesus about being in God's eternal kingdom. Jesus first pointed Nicodemus to look back at how God has acted with his people throughout history. By doing so, Nicodemus would have a solid foundation for his faith affirmation in this inquiry. Jesus asked Nicodemus, "Do you remember how Moses lifted up the serpent in the wilderness as a sign of God's power with the wandering Hebrews in the wilderness?" Each Passover, God's people relived the exodus. They remembered how they were called into being as God's people for a special mission to be fulfilled. They always lived in the hope that that deliverance would happen over and over again in their current situations. In others words, it was the revealed character of God and his steadfast love, compassion, mercy, and promises toward them that provided the anchor for their hope and peace in any wanting, longing situations along their journeys.

If the anchor gave the Israelites hope, then what Jesus told Nicodemus was the sure affirmation of his peace. Jesus said to Nicodemus, "Just as Moses lifted up the serpent in the wilderness, so must the Son of Man be lifted up, that whoever believes in him may have eternal life" (John 3:14–15). Whoever hears and sees this light of truth in Jesus, that person already knows his or her anchor in life, that he or she has the gift of eternal life in God's kingdom. Like that favorite hymn assures us, "Have no fear, little flock. It is the Father's good pleasure to give us the kingdom!" If the anchor was in some measure a feature of the hope in God's people under the first covenant, then the same is true for God's people under the second covenant through Jesus. That is what Jesus's answer told Nicodemus. That is also the future joy now as the anchor for our being at peace in every generation around the globe until the end of time as we know it. In Jesus, our anchor is in a uniquely decisive historical event. It is in and through Jesus's life journey for us and for all people along his road to the cross, through the tomb, and to the resurrection of a new forever life. As Jesus is the Risen One, so, too, are we by sign, gift, blessing, and promise!

This is the turning point in the story of our peace, disrupted by questions, doubts, threatening fears, or whatever their cause. Apostle Paul preached to the Christians living around Corinth, "For if only in this life we have hope in Christ, we should be pitied more than anyone. But now Christ has been raised from the dead, the firstfruits of those who have fallen asleep. For since death came through a man, the resurrection of the dead also came through a man. For just as in Adam all die, so in Christ all will be made alive" (1 Cor. 15:19–22 NET). Here is the source of our new and living hope, our peace assured and calmed, out of which we ought to embrace daily life with joy and gratitude. Why? Because our past has been accepted in the anchor event of God being with us and for us, always and equally, in the reconciling love, forgiveness, and promises acted out in Jesus's life, death, and resurrection: "For God so loved the world that he gave his only Son… For God sent the Son into the world, not to condemn the world, but that the world might be saved through him" (John 3:16–17).

Back to the future joy now! Our present moments, our present days, however many in ticktock time, can be lived in the freedom, the confidence, and the peace anchored in Jesus's announcement to Nicodemus's inquiry that day. Jesus was telling Nicodemus not only for his good, but for ours and all people, that if he saw this truth in Jesus, he could joyfully know for sure that he was born again by gift and blessing through the life and mission of the very One he was asking his question. Nicodemus would then know that he was in God's future through Jesus by "being lifted up from the earth on the cross" for all people. Jesus was saying here to Nicodemus that we can see ourselves as the forgiven ones. Our future is thus secured along with Nicodemus's future for nothing can ever separate us from the love of God that has been revealed to us in the life of Jesus. We can see then that Jesus's whole life is a parable story for our own lives and our outcome at the end of the journey! Since Jesus is present in our lives for our secured future, we can live now in that future joy.

Our ultimate question, like Nicodemus's question, is based then on this good news. It has its element in the past, which I call an anchor. As a person enters a community of faith, they are supported in ways that unbelievers are not. In baptism, the guarantee of God's acts and gifts for all of his people is personally declared for the person. This inheritance is marked upon our forehead with the sign of Jesus's cross. It is as durable and lasting as a red-hot branding tool used on the cattle on my grandpa's farm. I have created a mantra that I often teach and I recite daily as a reminder of our new identity and blessing gift announced at our baptism:

> *I am! I am who I am!*
> *Who I am gives meaning to my name!*
> *Once I was a nobody! I am baptized!*
> *I am Spirit-filled! I am a special somebody!*
> *I am a Christ person!*

This was the promise of sharing in God's future, which Jesus pointed out to Nicodemus and we share to each other at the beginning of every worship celebration in "Jesus's name." The guarantee of our gifts and blessings through Christ's death and resurrection is received in every worship celebration, just like in the Lord's Supper. Indeed, our baptism initiates us as we grow into a full understanding of this grace. This initiation and blessing support and serve us as an anchor in the storms as we remember whose we are and the promise of our destiny at the end of our earthly journey. We must remember that God is for us, not against us, until we are welcomed home to share in God's future. We ought to remember the importance of God's Word by reading and meditating on the scriptures. Refresh and nourish yourself by participating in worship gatherings of your choice and share in the Lord's Supper. Jesus's special meal of bread and wine provides us the memory, the comfort, the forgiveness, the peace, and the love that we all need for abundant living, and sometimes through storms in our journey to ultimate peace!

In the anchor for this forever peace now, this future joy now, we can in faith, courage and gratitude confidently affirm along our life's daily course another one of my mantras that I recite daily and often, especially in stormy seasons in my life's journey:

*The light of God surrounds me.*
*The love of God enfolds me.*
*The strength of God sustains me.*
*The presence of God watches over me.*
*The resurrection Gift of God renews me.*
*Wherever I am, God is there!*

That is the future joy now! That is the future peace, calmed, renewed, and transformed forever! That is living daily with awareness, with assurance, and with peace, knowing that we are already now daughters and sons, like the risen Jesus, in God's kingdom. We will all be given the crown of life as royal princesses and princes, daughters and sons of the Prince of Peace who was born in a Bethlehem manager, Jesus of Nazareth.

## The Journey Verse

I have spoken these things to you while staying with you. But the Advocate, the Holy Spirit, whom the Father will send in my name, will teach you everything, and will cause you to remember everything I have said to you. "Peace I leave with you; my peace I give to you; I do not give it to you as the world does. Do not let your hearts be distressed or lacking in courage."

(John 14:25–27 NET)

# Chapter 9

# In the Turning Points with Wonderment

*Soon afterward he went to a town called Nain, and his disciples and a large crowd went with him. As he approached the gate of the town, a man who had died was being carried out—the only son of his mother, and she was a widow. And a large crowd from the town was with her. When the Lord saw her, his heart went out to her and he said, "Don't cry." Then he went up and touched the bier they were carrying him on, and the bearers stood still. He said, "Young man, I say to you, get up!" The dead man sat up and began to speak, and Jesus gave him back to his mother... This word about Jesus spread throughout Judea and the surrounding country.*
          —Luke 7:11–17 (NIV)

The last feeling to be discussed is wonderment. We share this feeling as a natural gift within our designed image of the Creator (Gen. 1:27). The God we know expressed wonderment over what had been created each day or in each eon, for a day is a thousand years and a thousand years is a day, as a psalmist said. As each day was completed, the Creator declared in joy, "It is good." (Gen. 1:31).

We see in one of Jesus's parables another kind of wonderment expressed by the Creator through Jesus. At the beginning of chapter 18 in Luke, Jesus compares the vindication by an unrighteous judge with God's vindication. What is God's vindication like? It is a vindication without delay and torture. God elected Jesus to vindicate us as his daughters and sons. Remember the promise in John 3:17, "Indeed, God did not send the Son into the world to condemn the world, but in order that the world might be saved through him." As this story is remembered for each of us in our deserved judgment, God will act speedily. This is the foundation for our faith in all the situations and turning points of wonderment along life's journey. What's next? What is going to happen? Are we good enough? Are we worthy by our efforts, by our good works? What is in store for us in the ultimate turning point at the end? What are your wonderments? The good news in God's vindication is that Jesus's story counts as our "wedding garment" so that we can be free guests in the future household of God made whole and new forever. Jesus's story covers the pages of our stories, good and bad, with God's unconditional love and forgiveness. Forgiveness is faith's experience of a liberating vindication that makes us heirs with Jesus in God's timeless future.

Jesus begins this parable with an admonition for our faith journey. We are pointed toward the practice of prayer in all of life's major and minor turning points. Followers in Jesus's way pray persistently through their journey, especially in any wonderment experiences and situations. We should not lose heart from the challenges and tests of endurance, even in such frightful threats and tragedies caused by the COVID-19 pandemic. Housebound due to the shutdowns, we can only watch on the daily news while families and friends get infected around us. Jesus teaches in his parables that we must not lose heart from the challenges and sufferings along the way to sharing life in God's future. Jesus closes his teaching on vindication, the parable of the widow and the unjust judge (Luke 18:1–8), with a question. The question reflects another kind of feeling that is present in us. Wonderment is another gift in our birth package. This feeling of wonderment is seen in Jesus's question, "When the Son of Man comes, will he find faith on earth?" (Luke 18:8).

I can personally identify with Jesus's wonderment in this question. Some years ago, I remember being asked to give the prayer invocation at a dinner meeting for a professional association. A man sitting beside me wasted no time in telling me that he did not believe in God. He said that he saw no need for such a prayer. It did make me wonder, *What am I doing here?* Furthermore, he stated, "This life is all there is! Get out of life what you can for death is man's exit into nothingness." This conversation, which did not end on that comment, brought back to my inner thoughts the question that kept passing through my mind as I returned to Perrysburg, Ohio, from my boyhood Slater farm community in central Iowa just a couple of weeks earlier. I was returning to my home after attending my brother Dean's funeral. My brother, who taught me to play baseball and basketball and to be a master carpenter and woodworker, had died from a rare kidney disease in his early fifties.

I was wondering about this same question I was confronted with at the dinner meeting, "After death, then what?" I can imagine that if we were to take a survey for topics of greatest concern and wonderment that confront us, this ultimate wonderment would be near the top of the list. Death, from our human point of view, is no doubt one of the most important turning points that we face in life. This question is made crucial by the certainty that all of us must go through this turning point, regardless of what that exit might be. One thing we know for sure is that today we are alive. From our human point of view, the only sure thing any of us really has is each day that we awake, and the flow of the moments as that day unfolds. Someday we shall pass to naught as far as this time-space world is experienced. This question is made crucial also by the fact that loved ones, as precious to us as life itself, pass into the unknown that Jesus called "like unto a sleep." The loss of a loved one of any age—from an infant to a middle-aged spouse, a family member or friend in their golden years—to an illness, an accident, or a strange new virus like the COVID-19 makes no difference in the ultimate wonderment question, What is next, if anything, after death?

In Luke chapter 7, Jesus raised the son of the widow from Nain:

*And when the Lord saw her, he had compassion on her and said to her, "Do not weep." Then he came up and touched the bier, and the bearers stood still. And he said, "Young man, I say to you, arise." And the dead man sat up and began to speak, and Jesus gave him to his mother.* (Luke 7:13–15 ESV)

When those closest to us die, we face the wonderment of life's destiny. I have no way of knowing the thoughts passing through the mind of the widow from Nain nor what her friends were thinking or perhaps saying to her to comfort her during the funeral procession that day. From my understanding of human reactions and feelings during such a turning point in decades of pastoral ministry, then I think I am safe in projecting that they, too, were concerned with this question of what awaits after death.

If we are open and true about sharing our feelings, our wonderments and hopes, one cannot be indifferent to the fate of another person whose life has given true meaning to our own life. When the woman from Nain lost her husband, she ceased to be a wife. When she lost her only son, perhaps she ceased to be a mother. These relationships gave her meaning and purpose in life. Now that she was alone, she would weep.

There are many other wonderments in our turning points before the ultimate one. I am quite safe in projecting that to some degree, all of us are apprehensive about developments in this country and around the world in the first two decades of the 2000s. They are manifested in the tensions and division within our country and between the nations around the globe, from the disrespect for our NATO allies and important political issues like nuclear weapons and environmental treaties. The trade wars, especially with China and neighboring countries, has caused the prices to skyrocket for medicines, clothing, food, tools, spare parts, and other such essential products from outside of our country. This had a negative impact on family farms, businesses large and small, and on our everyday consumption and living patterns.

Where is all this going? What is next for us, for our children and their children? We hear the death rattles for much of that which has been a part of our daily lives as we wonder what the brave new world is going to look like. We wonder during this unprecedented situation of the COVID-19 shutdown, mass unemployment, and our stay-at-home directives that now promise to continue through the summer months and perhaps well into the fall of 2020 and for months into 2021, what will be the drastic changes in employment offices and work places, in our schools and college classrooms, in our favorite restaurants and coffee shops, and in our grocery stores and shopping malls? How will these work? Will social spaces and even buildings be redesigned to prepare for the next spike in the pandemic attack or another new global viral attack? We faced this frightening experience daily with a host of questions: When will COVID-19 be fully understood in its makeup, source, and transfer patterns? When will an effective vaccine be discovered and manufactured for global distribution? When can all forms of employment and businesses be opened and safely be operational? When will school classes and doctor's appointments no longer be by iPhone video? What wonderment do you remember from your experiences with the COVID-19 pandemic?

We see all around us signs of the birth pangs to come, yet it is not clear what that will be. If what we are experiencing is not creating times of confusion, tension, confrontation, refocusing our dreams, and adjusting our lifestyles, then it is at least creating wonderment for individuals and families, for towns and cities of all sizes, for businesses and corporations, and for all nations around the globe. In our situations of wonderment, the first thing that needs to be said about a life rooted in Jesus is that commitment must come before belief, not belief before commitment! Life for such changing times and major turning points along the way must always start where biblical faith starts. We see this in Jesus's calling his first disciples to follow him and to learn from him. Likewise, we see this in Jesus's order to his disciples, "Go therefore and make disciples of all nations, baptizing them in the name of the Father and of the Son and of the Holy

Spirit, and teaching them to obey everything that I have commanded you" (Matt. 28:19–20).

Biblical faith starts with daily commitment to the leading of the Lord. Our model starts with Abraham who responded to a calling that unfolded through many experiences of wonderment:

> *Now the Lord said to Abram, "Go from your country and your kindred and your father's house to the land that I will show you. And I will make of you a great nation (through many turning points—wars, famines, apostasy, apathy, confusion, and emptiness), and I will bless you and make your name great, so that you will be a blessing."* (Gen. 12:1–2 ESV)

Jesus affirmed that same model of commitment before faith. We walk with Jesus into a fuller understanding of the Way, the Truth, and the Life of abundant living and our destiny in God's future:

> *Passing alongside the Sea of Galilee, he saw Simon and Andrew the brother of Simon casting a net into the sea, for they were fisherman. And Jesus said to them, "Follow me, and I will make you become fishers of men."… And going a little further, he saw James the son of Zebedee and John his brother, who were in their boats mending nets. And immediately he called them… And as he passed by, he saw Levi the son of Alphaeus sitting at the tax booth, and he said to them, "Follow me."* (Mark 1:16–17, 19–20, 2:14 ESV)

This response is a commitment. It is the beginning in the life of faith that has no ending. The calling is an act of grace. The journey is under grace. The future destiny is a gift of grace. With the baptism of water, Jesus is saying to all of us, "Live in me! Follow me! Follow my Way, my Truth, and my Life! I will give you a purpose for living and an example of your ending. You are free to create your plan and to live it, but remember that I am with you always! You shall rise as I am risen!"

Apostle Paul followed suit and advocated the same, "Therefore as you received Christ Jesus the Lord, so walk in him, rooted and built up in him and established in the faith" (Col. 2:6–7 ESV). These words imply continuous development and progress in our faith as we walk in openness with the Spirit, leading us into the truth and fullness of God's way in the kingdom that is to come. The Holy Spirit dwelling within us enables us to believe in all things and hope for all things Jesus taught, even in our times of struggle and suffering. That Spirit enables us to learn, cope, endure, and start over from our mistakes and failures. The good news is that our past is accepted under God's love and grace. Today is a new day with new possibilities! Our tomorrow is another today until we are in God's timeless eternity beyond calendar days. Our future is secured for us in the gift of God's eternity.

Our walk with the Living Word in faith does not ring shallow or is limited by our human wisdom, philosophy, and projections. Such faith is adequate for times of wonderment and change. Change is constant until history reaches its goal. Easter is a sign that God is on the side of life and will make all things new. The global COVID-19 pandemic came upon us like a tsunami that caused drastic disruptions and changes in all our lives, communities, and countries. As we seek a cure to this virus, we hope it will be available as soon as possible. The ultimate solution to such problems, threats, and conditions is the final victory, even those caused by the COVID-19 virus. It will be the same victory as the one on the cross and in the empty tomb, making all things whole and new.

Within ourselves and our experiences, wonderment takes on different forces, as we see in some of the role models in the gospel:

- *For Nicodemus, it was a loss of identity.* "What can I do to get a new start in life?" This is often the cry of our inner self.

- *For Zacchaeus, it was his emptiness and loneliness despite his vast wealth.* "What is salvation, the way that leads to fullness of life?" How often do we cling to counterfeit treasures?
- *For Mary Magdalene, it was the social rejection and the threat of death.* "Where is there a law, a word that heals rather than kills?" We continue to look for acceptance and support.
- *For Lazarus and his sisters Mary and Martha, it was the death of their brother and the absent Lord who could have altered the situation.* "Why were you not here in our struggle and our need, Lord?"
- *For the disciples, it was the situation in the garden of Gethsemane.* "Why not destroy these enemies with the sword?" Violent acts are still chosen and expressed as the way through many wonderments, to suppress them, to control them, to destroy others we do not like, understand, or want in our lives.
- For Jesus, it was praying all night in the garden of Gethsemane before his arrest and final journey to the cross event where he cried, "My God, my God, why have you forsaken me?" This is the cry of many human hearts in crises.

We find similarities in these stories with our own experiences. We can identify with all of these turning points. They mirror our needs and wonderments. In these situations, Jesus is a source of renewing power, of strength and peace, of healing and transformation, and of new beginnings. Jesus's word remains the same for us today and in every generation, "Follow me! Live anew daily in my light and in my way! Let your life be rooted and built up in me!" We see here the difference Jesus can make in our turning points. We are not alone. Jesus promises, "I will not leave you desolate; I will come to you" (John 14:18 RSV) and "And I will pray the Father, and he will give you another Counselor, to be with you for ever, even the Spirit of truth, whom the world cannot receive, because it neither sees him nor knows him; you know him, for he dwells with you, and will be in you" (John 14:16–17 RSV). Jesus raised this concern we each must wrestle and be personally responsible if we are going to live daily with inner strength. Jesus closes the scene with his own wonderment question, "when the Son of Man comes, will he find faith on earth?" (Luke 18:8)

Far too many people want to live their faith-life, if they affirm one, in relationship to historical facts covered with the dust of the centuries. For some, their faith is based on feelings they have attached to man-made interpretations and traditions from the past or based on current philosophies and cultural fads. These foundations can give a false sense of security and are often found wanting in the wonderment struggles and sufferings that come into our lives, causing immense disruptions in our peace and security, as manifested by the COVID-19 virus spreading across the United States and around the globe. In response, they often abandon their faith, suppressing or rejecting the gift of faith within themselves, at least until a reawakening. They may turn to destructive behaviors and perhaps even to drugs or alcohol to escape from their life's situations. Though wisdom and understanding is helpful in the faith journey, it is not the basis. It is personal relationship and commitment! Jesus's parable comparing the unrighteous judge and the vindicating God of Creation ends, as we have noted several times in this chapter, with that question of wonderment: "when the Son of Man comes, will he find faith on earth?" Not just commitment to tradition, human wisdom, or to one's feelings about one's chosen beliefs.

From biblical role models, we should be living our life with the presence of Jesus who echoes the same call, "Follow me!" Indeed, we must follow him through the bright and joyous moments, through the dark and tragic crises of the day, or through whatever experiences or situations around you (daily news). Jesus tells all of us to have a personal relationship with him and to follow him until we could be reunited with God at a place where all things are whole and new forever.

It is helpful and important to remember that even the scribes and Pharisees in Jesus's day were divided on the wonderment of a relationship beyond the grave. I cannot help but wonder if the widow of Nain was not grasping for an answer to that basic question about life after death. In fact, we do not know much else about this woman. Her story is one of my favorite stories in the gospels because of my own pressing need throughout my life's journey to know the answer to the ultimate wonderment question. This became a pressing issue when my life and future was threatened by stage 4 melanoma as I was approaching forty years old. There is no mention of the woman from Nain having great faith or even a confession that moved Jesus to compassion and to manifest his life-giving power. In the scene, we find only a weeping crowd following the coffin bearers with the widow's dead son. Jesus's action that day marked the presence of a new hope for one's faith in all seasons and turning points. Our Savior acted with power in a historical moment to show in a symbolic way the answer to the ultimate question of what happens after death.

Life ends not in death or nothingness as the man told me at that dinner where I gave a prayer invocation. Life ends in new life with Jesus. All the old traditions or ideas about the dead were now challenged. As Jesus moved toward the funeral coffin, he broke a Jewish tradition found in the book of Numbers. Such an action was forbidden. If anyone in a funeral procession touched the bier, he or she became unclean and banished from the community until he or she had gone through the proper steps of purification.

Jesus shattered any traditional notions concerning this question. He certainly did not call the young man back to life only so that he could return to work to support his widowed mother or weep with his friends in times of sorrow and crisis. The young man was not called back to life only to experience final death again. It would be cruelty beyond reason if Jesus was only exercising some magical act in bringing the boy back to life. Jesus did not resurrect the woman's son so that he could experience the pain and struggle of death again. He did it so we would follow him in faith through the generations. It was done so that the Son of Man would save us when the end time comes. Jesus spoke the words "Young man, I say to you, rise!" in order to make known, in their present time, the new age to come and the power of his resurrection for all people when one day he would again touch the whole Creation, as he touched the funeral bier in the village of Nain, to make all things new. It will be that time when we will be granted our inheritance, the gift of life anew in God's eternal future. The record of this resurrection and Jesus's part in it speaks to the basic wonderments that you and I face throughout life.

What is the meaning of life? What is the meaning of death? We realize, it seems almost instinctively, that the deepest meaning of life is determined by what we believe about death and the future. Nevertheless, making sense of life means, ultimately, making sense of death. It is quite true that the whole point of a journey is determined by the destination. If the future or destination only holds blank nothingness, then our daily life has lost its focus, its deeper meaning, and its greater value. There would be no need for the kind of faith Jesus hopes to see on the earth. Many people live in this emptiness and meaninglessness today, especially in the twenty-first century, as so many values, norms, and institutions have degenerated or been abandoned. They are forced to concede that it makes no real difference how they live day by day. Some seek this nothingness on their own when life becomes too unbearable. All respect for human life is finally lost. Personhood is devalued. People make themselves gods. Many become selfish, exploiting other people and every situation in life for their own ends.

An unknown soldier once addressed this wonderment that weighs upon our feelings and faith:

> *If it be all for naught, for nothingness at last,*
> *Why does God make the world so fair?*
> *Why set this hunger for eternity*
> *To gnaw my heartstrings through if death ends all?*
> *If death ends all, then evil must be good,*
> *Wrong must be right, and beauty must be ugliness.*
> *God is a Judas who betrays his Son,*
> *And with a kiss, damns all the world to hell*
> *If Christ rose not again!*

Christ has risen indeed! Every new day is an Easter morning. The risen Jesus, the Spirit of Life is with us and for us on our life's journey until we are with our Creator forever. Indeed, we are Easter people in this Good Friday kind of world. That is our basis and anchor for facing, embracing, handling, and struggling through our wonderments along life's journey.

## The Journey Verse

But now thus says the Lord, he who created you, O Jacob, he who formed you, O Israel: "Fear not, for I have redeemed you; I have called you by name, you are mine. When you pass through the waters, I will be with you; and through the rivers, they shall not overwhelm you; when you walk through the fire you shall not be burned, and the flame shall not consume you. For I am the Lord your God, the Holy One of Israel, your Savior. I give Egypt as your ransom, Cush and Seba in exchange for you. Because you are precious in my eyes, and honored, and I love you.

(Isaiah 43:1–4 ESV)

# Chapter 10

# The Secret Is Out:
# The Faith That Counts!

*After Jesus had finished teaching all this to the people, he entered Capernaum. A centurion there had a slave who was highly regarded, but who was sick and at the point of death. When the centurion heard about Jesus, he sent some Jewish elders to him, asking him to come and heal his slave. When they came to Jesus, they urged to him earnestly, "He is worthy to have you do this for him, because he loves our nation, and even built our synagogue." So Jesus went with them. When he was not far from the house, the centurion sent friends to say to him, "Lord, do not trouble yourself, for I am not worthy to have you come under my roof! That is why I did not presume to come to you. Instead, say the word, and my servant must be healed."... When Jesus heard this, he was amazed at him. He turned and said to the crowd that followed him, "I tell you, not even in Israel have I found such faith!" So when those who had been sent returned to the house, they found the slave well.*

—Luke 7:1–7, 9–10 (NET)

We have reflected on nine natural feelings that are in our birth package as individuals created in the image of God. These feelings are neutral until expressed. They are positive when used in good and just ways. Feelings are an essential part of our healthy well-being. They are to be affirmed and expressed in abundant living. We have observed how these feelings are seen in the Old Testament and in the Living Word embodied in Jesus of Nazareth (John 1:1–5, 14). All feelings can be experienced negatively and expressed in destructive ways toward oneself, others, and even toward God. Have you done this? Have you seen or experienced this?

In this final chapter, we turn to an exposed secret, reflecting on the "faith that counts" in all seasons and circumstances along life's journey. It has been said that life is a series of choices. Even our cells had to choose in their embryonic stage what they were going to be as they gave form and shape to a unique human being. Our cells had to choose their special roles in the formation of the various organs, muscles, and tissues. From our infancy, we learn to cry or not to cry, to sleep or not to sleep, to want food or not to want food, to keep booties on or to kick booties off, and to crawl or not to crawl. Choices! Choices! Choices! As the years pass, the numerous choices continue daily, some easier and some more difficult: to wear the same color of socks to school or not, to do all the homework or not, to take piano lessons or to play a musical instrument, to play sports or work at the local café, to get body art and piercings or not, to take someone to the school dance or stay home, and to like someone or not? There is that popular saying, "Not to decide is to decide!"

Indeed, God designed us with free wills. Part of the journey of maturing is to learn to use our free will to make good choices and acts. Our life story is a series and collection of choices. These choices all have an impact and significance on the quality, outcome, satisfaction, and fulfillment as well the destruction of one's life in each stage. Learning solid information early in life and in every stage of life becomes important for one's choices. Besides our feelings, we have another special gift within ourselves to recognize and affirm each day along our life's journey, the gift of faith. Martin Luther taught in his many writings that the first gift of the Spirit abiding in us is faith. When we become aware of it, we are aware of the abiding Spirit's presence in us. The supportive, guiding work of the Spirit of Life is seen in the fruits of the Spirit manifested through each of our unique personalities: love, joy, peace, patience, kindness, generosity, faithfulness, gentleness, and self-control (Gal. 5:22–23).

Faith is not something that we create in ourselves or acquired by our own effort and understanding. We may learn, uphold, affirm, and defend a set of traditions or beliefs. Beliefs may not always reflect faithfulness. Beliefs may not always reflect in their practice the fruits of the Spirit with integrity toward all people. It is not faith that saves us, but faith in God and his Son Jesus who saved us and will save all the generations (John 3:16–17). It is our free choice to recognize and affirm, to nurture and express faith as a natural gift of the Spirit or to deny it. This gift may be latent within us until there is an awakening caused by some need or crisis. We have an illustration of this truth present within each of us, all created in the image of God. By free choice, it can be expressed and acted out in daily life, especially in times of crisis such as the COVID-19 pandemic.

The account of Jesus healing a centurion's servant, among other accounts, demonstrates this truth. This recorded incident involves two leaders of power and authority. It involves a military and political leader in the centurion, representing Rome in the region of Capernaum. It also involves Jesus, representing the powers and promises of God's kingdom on earth. The centurion, a powerful man, was concerned about the health of one of his servants. Remembering the centurion's political position, it might be more accurate for us to think of this person as a close loyal helper. He was like the centurion's assistant. The central focus in the account is not the miracle of the healing, but the miracle of faith by the centurion. It is significant to point out here that centurion was not even an Israelite, God's chosen people. He was not a member in the Capernaum synagogue, but the caring, loving, and generous donor of the new building. The fact that the centurion's helper had a terminal illness serves to heighten the anticipated demonstration of the greater authority, the greater power present in Jesus. When the centurion heard about Jesus and his presence in the centurion's territorial region, the centurion, by his own recognition, affirmation, and choice, sent for Jesus to heal his dying servant.

We begin to see this truth clearly in this outsider governing in Capernaum. The centurion is demonstrating the faith that counts in this life's journey and its daily needs and crises. When Jesus heard this about the centurion and his request to heal his dying servant, Jesus obliged. When Jesus heard about the centurion's faith, he was amazed at him. Turning to his own disciples and the crowd following him, Jesus said, "I tell you, not even in Israel have I found such faith" (Luke 7:9). Unlike many career officers who commanded military garrisons in the occupied countries in Jesus's day, he was compassionate toward his assistant. This centurion was reverent toward the Jewish community and their elders. We are told that he built a new synagogue for them. He sent the elders to Jesus as emissaries of mercy. He was humble before Jesus. When Jesus neared the centurion's house for this miracle healing, the centurion sent some of his friends to Jesus with a message, "Lord, do not trouble yourself, for I am not worthy to have you come under my roof. Therefore I did not presume to come to you. But say the word, and let my servant be healed" (Luke 7:6–7 ESV).

Here we see the faith that counts! This centurion recognized Jesus to be of higher authority than his own Roman authority. He is a man of authority. Whatever he says to his people, they do it. Yet he recognizes Jesus's authority over his authority, saying, "Jesus, just say the healing word from where you are now. I have faith in you! It will happen." It is this point in the story that becomes even more important to us. It tells us about the faith that counts to Jesus of Nazareth and to God! The centurion first sent a delegation of Jewish elders to Jesus, seeking the healing that his servant desperately needed. Even that act marks this centurion a person of unusual sensitivity. In the ancient world, a slave was valued no higher than a piece of real estate, special or not. This soldier's concern for another person, the humility of his approach to Jesus, and his spiritual discernment are all examples worthy of note in his personality traits, but it was his faith that counted!

The centurion's faith was recognized and affirmed by Jesus. It prompted Jesus's act of healing. The centurion was an outsider, not from the household of Israel, the prevalent institution of faith in that region in Jesus's day. Jesus marveled at the simplicity of this man's faith (Luke 7:9). The centurion needed the authority, power, and benefits of God in this situation. He needed what he recognized, accepted, and affirmed was possible with the words spoken by Jesus. In faith, the centurion turned to Jesus for authority and power that he did not have within himself. The centurion only had the faith that counts. Knowing the need of his dying servant, his faith prompted him to seek out Jesus to heal his servant. The faith of the centurion was a discernment of Jesus's authority and a simple trust in it. The faith that counts does involve discernments, simple trust, and daily acts that express that faith with love. It is here that this story becomes a lesson for all of us. Just like the centurion at his political and military post in Capernaum, even the strongest, the most self-reliant, and the most dedicated of God's people and all outsiders of that household, and we today in modern times, all eventually need something that only Jesus can give.

My prayer for all of us from the story of the centurion is, "Yes, Lord Jesus, keep on saying your healing words, your helping words, and your guiding words to those who have eyes to see and ears to hear. Yes, Lord Jesus, keep those who have the faith that counts, daily affirming their faith with love. Lord Jesus, awaken that faith more and more in those who are asleep to that gift or living in denial of that gift within themselves that they might live abundantly in your way." When we come in humility in times of special needs for ourselves and others, asking Jesus for help, we can be sure that God's presence, authority, power, and action to meet our needs will be there for our help, as it was for the centurion and his servant. We see a special lesson here in the return of the Jewish elders and the centurion's friends to his residence. They found the servant healed and doing well, yet no specific command of healing was recorded. Not even a word was necessary. The centurion did not require one. He hoped, he waited, and he trusted! Such faith secured the benefit in due time. There was no marveling over the miracle of healing in this story.

Luke wants us to focus on the greater miracle—the faith that counts! What is this *faith that counts*? What is this faith that amazes and moves our Lord Jesus to respond joyously and act to fulfill our needs? The responsive acts may not be as immediate as we want. They may come over time. Jesus's response to our needs may give us something different or better for us.

Let me acknowledge here that it is not my intention to present in this chapter a boxed answer to this question. There is no fixed formula that can quickly address all our questions about faith and doubts, about joys and disappointments, and about blessings and sufferings. For many, the doubts, disappointments, and sufferings often blocks faith from being affirmed and trusted, and blocks faith from giving the strength of hope and endurance. Even the centurion in Capernaum had to wait, hope, and trust for Jesus to heal his servant. We have all lived under those fixed formulas that can carry us along in the sunny seasons of life. We know those sayings and perhaps we have uttered them in situations in our daily life: "Faith can do anything!" "If you only have enough faith, you can move mountains!" "Faith is always victorious!" and "If you have enough faith, it will carry you through the despair in your life!" In these sayings, faith is seen as something more or something less. It is seen as a quantity that we possess, manage, and control.

The secret is out! The faith that counts is God's gift within us. It is not more or less in quantity. We do not possess it as if we are managers of something. We do not control the gift. We have the gift and can choose to live by it and act from it. We can recognize it, live with it, and express it in our daily living. It is the gift of the abiding Spirit within us, prompting, supporting, guiding, and working in and through us in our journey (Gal. 5:22–23). It is Jesus keeping his promise to us in all seasons and situations (Matt. 28:20). At the end of our personal time on this earthly journey, the risen Jesus and the Creator will be there to welcome us home with exceedingly great joy!

From these shallow sayings, perhaps we continue to harbor false notions about faith. This understanding of faith and its payoff that we hold and affirm as true, often over against what someone else advocates, somehow connects us to God in such a way that our journey is one great big slide on skids that are always greased. God is real and faith is real when everything is smooth sliding. I doubt that everything else was going smooth in the centurion's life in his post in Capernaum, except for his favorite servant being ill unto death. I doubt that everything was smooth going even after Jesus healed his servant. There was no condition or quantity, more or less. There was no personal self-worth, power, or control behind his affirmation of Jesus as Lord and his prayer request (Luke 7:7). That is the faith that counts! The temptation for us when things do not slide along that smoothly in our wants or needs is we wonder where God and the abiding Spirit of Jesus are now. Why the delay? Why the absence? How is God meeting our needs, hopes, and longings? Is God helping, healing, or changing our situations on our behalf or for someone special in our family, friends, or community? We begin to doubt that we have faith.

Here we are again, back to faith being a quantity that we either possess or do not possess. Some people understand faith as something we acquire with our own reason, power, or strength from our study and understanding. We can gain wisdom, insights, and beliefs by self-study or from mentors, but such efforts do not necessarily lead us to faith. Wisdom and packages of beliefs do not necessarily lead us to the recognition and affirmation of the faith that counts. They do not necessarily lead to open awareness and trust in the abiding Spirit of the risen Christ who will welcome all of us home to our eternal future in God's Creation with exceedingly great joy, whole and new forever.

What we learn from the centurion's experience with the healing of his servant by Jesus is that faith is simply the gift within each of us as created by God. It is that openness to be aware of and responsive to the abiding presence of the Spirit of Life in us as the centurion was open and responsive to Jesus in his situation that day. It is our acceptance and affirmation of Jesus present in our lives and in our circumstances, even when we have to cry out like Jesus did on the cross: "My God, my God, why have you forsaken me?" (Matt. 27:46). In the centurion's situation, faith is shown as simply trusting in the authority, compassion, love, and powers of Jesus. It was not the centurion's character, status, authority, power, or adherence to religious knowledge that amazed Jesus. It was his faith that counted. It moved Jesus to heal his servant. The centurion had enough faith to say Jesus did not have to come to his house, but just say the word and his servant will be healed. That is real faith! That is the faith at which Jesus marvels. Likewise, we are not saved, healed, or resurrected by our faith in our faith, by our particular brand of religious knowledge and beliefs, whether we are insiders or outsiders in a religious group, community, or nation. We are healed, saved, resurrected by Jesus of Nazareth.

Many people think that faith is something they have or acquire through their own efforts, studies, and reasoning. For the centurion, faith was a simple openness to who Jesus was and what Jesus could do for him and his servant. It was a confession of Jesus's authority and power being greater than his own and even greater than the authority and power of the Roman Empire the centurion represented and served in Capernaum. It was a recognition of a condition in this servant that he could do nothing about with all the knowledge, powers, and national resources of Rome at his disposal. It was simply a trust in Jesus. It was the faith that counts! When things do not quite work out and requests are not met, many people conclude that their faith is not strong enough. Perhaps they conclude that God is not on their side and no longer cares about their personal needs and wishes. Then they are bound to despair and may even deny or reject faith altogether; that is, to deny or to reject the very Lord of Creation who is waiting for us to call him while keeping his promise to us (Matt. 28:20).

In the centurion's story, the faith that counts is a condition of readiness in one's life to receive what God wants to give to us either now or at life's end when we each are presented before the throne of grace by Jesus, the risen Lord. Faith involves our acceptance of wanting and waiting, of needing and hoping, of receiving and not receiving, and of knowing and not knowing. In this story, we see the affirmation that God's lordship is greater than the authority, power, and resources of Rome, in Washington DC, Beijing, or Moscow. Political power may establish and keep order for decades or centuries. It may even provide the ways and means for a new synagogue like the centurion built for the Jewish community in Capernaum. It may provide for a vaccine to neutralize the global threat that is the COVID-19 pandemic. However, political power cannot provide resources and solutions for many of our needs as soon as we need them. It cannot provide for the ultimate need, life after death. It took the faith that counts and the presence of Jesus, the Lord over death, to provide the healing needed by the centurion's dying servant in Capernaum.

The great lesson for us in the centurion's story is that even the finest, the most able and upright, and the most powerful human beings we know still need God. Both Jews and Gentiles, like the centurion, need God. Without God, their lives can never be complete, healed, or restored anew to life beyond death. Their lives can never achieve their highest witness, highest good, highest purpose, or highest service through their journey days. This faith of the centurion was even a higher witness than his public acts that made the new synagogue possible in Capernaum. The centurion recognized and acted on his faith that counts. He was open to the one he recognized and called the Lord. He knew that Jesus could do something for him that he himself could not do despite all his authority and power, his inner strength and goodness, and his compassion and love. This centurion had a situation beyond his own ability to manage, conquer, or change. Sometimes it takes a real crisis to bring the faith that counts out of us.

Jesus is always present with us, waiting to be amazed and marvel over us to see the faith that counts. He is waiting to say about you and me, "I tell you, not even in Israel have I found such faith" (Luke7:9). The Spirit of the Living God is present even through this time and place, wherever I am and wherever you are as you read this book. The Spirit of Life, that abides in us and with us along our journey days, calls all of us into the current of where God is going with history. The Spirit of Life seeks to work out in and through us that abundant life that was acted out and accomplished in and through Jesus the Christ. Those who are open and allow this Spirit to work in their gifts of feelings and faith will know that God is alive. They will recognize God's presence in them and will affirm and express the faith that counts, the faith that bears us with joy, strength, peace, and hope along life's journey until we arrive in our new home with God forever. Behold, the gifts of your feelings and faith! Affirm and express them freely, abundantly, and joyfully along your life's journey.

## The Journey Verse

May you lead lives worthy of the Lord, fully pleasing to him, as you bear fruit in every good work and as you grow in the knowledge of God. May you be made strong with all the strength that comes from his glorious power, and may you be prepared to endure everything with patience, while joyfully giving thanks to the Father, who has enabled you to share in the inheritance of the saints in the light. He has rescued us from the power of darkness and transferred us into the kingdom of his beloved Son, in whom we have redemption, the forgiveness of sins.

(Colossians 1:10–14 NRSV)

# About the Author

Louis W. Accola has been a pastor, preacher, teacher, and counselor. He is the author of several books and numerous resources for church members and church councils used for leadership and mission development. He shared these resources in workshops and retreats nationally as a trainer and mentor.

Accola is a nationally recognized writer of resources on prayer patterns for spiritual formation and a facilitator for spirituality retreats. As the national director of parish development for the former American Lutheran Church, he was a recognized leader for decades in the Worship Renewal and in the Ecumenical Church Renewal Movements. He also served as pastor, teacher, and counselor at parishes in Waterloo, Iowa; Milwaukee, Wisconsin; Perrysburg, Ohio; and Woodinville, Washington. Before retirement, he served for a decade as pastor for spiritual formation and pastoral care at Prince of Peace Lutheran Church in Phoenix, Arizona.

The author holds a bachelor's degree from Luther College in Decorah, Iowa and graduated summa cum laude. He also holds a master's degree from Luther Seminary at St. Paul, Minnesota and from Princeton Seminary in Princeton, New Jersey; and a doctorate from McCormick Theological Seminary in Chicago, Illinois, all of which he graduated from with highest honors.

Accola is a son of an Iowa farm family. Growing up in the heartland, he was nurtured to be a lover, helper, and caretaker of plants, animals, and all living creatures in God's awesome creation along life's journey. He is also a minister, counselor, biblical student, and devoted teacher. He is a lover of the creative arts and a master ceramist, teaching ceramics in his retirement community while spending winters in Mesa, Arizona.

The author has four sons, Terence, Hans, Steven, and Kent, and a daughter named Katie. He lives with his journey companion and wife Kathy, a mother, nurse educator, and writer, and their dog Lexi, in Woodinville, Washington.

CPSIA information can be obtained
at www.ICGtesting.com
Printed in the USA
FSHW010159131021
85358FS